Love, Wine, and Vengeance

A *Dr. Mary Paul in Florida* Mystery

Mary F. Kohnke

Love, Wine, and Vengeance

A *Dr. Mary Paul in Florida* Mystery

Mary F. Kohnke

New Dimensions Projects

Ponte Vedra Beach, Florida

Love, Wine, and Vengeance

This book is a work of fiction.
Any resemblance to any person, living or dead,
is completely coincidental.

Cover design: Kip Williams
Cover photo: Shutterstock

For information contact
New Dimensions Projects, P.O. Box 1213,
Ponte Vedra Beach, Fl 32004.

Published 2016
Printed in the United States of America
09 08 07 10 9 8 7 6 5 4 3 2

Cataloging-in-Publication Data
Love, Wine, and Vengeance / Mary F. Kohnke - 1st Ed
p. cm

"A Dr. Mary Paul in Florida Mystery"

ISBN 978-0-92774536-8-9
ISBN 10: 0-9774536-8-5

1. Murder -Sonoma California-Fiction
2. Women-Politics Florida -Fiction
3. Vineyards and Wine- Fiction
4. International Crime Syndicate-Fiction
5. Dressage Riding-Fiction

PS3626.64 2016 813.54 -dc22
Library of Congress Control Number
2016952429

Author's Notes

My research for this book began in the library, reading every-thing I could find on the making of champagne and port. The champagne section was especially difficult. I sent these sections to Mr. Brent Burkey, a man with some knowledge on wines, to see if I made the subject understandable yet reasonably accurate. I also did not want to bore the reader.

He laughed and said my simplification of the the difficulty of the process was fine, even if I did stretch the writer's freedom of artistic license a bit. (I thought that was a nice way to put it.) I thank this very nice, very bright man.

The subject matter of the book is in three areas: Holidays and love In Sonoma; learning how to create two difficult wines; and then back to Florida to find closure in death.

Most important, I am indebted to Mr. Kip Williams. He did the editing and design, putting pieces together and helping in creating the cover. He is, as usual, very fine, patient, and understands that books are people's babies. He corrects with great delicacy.

As usual there are many characters, so the descriptions page is long. If you have read my other books these will be old friends to you. Again, let me invite you to pour a glass of wine, sit in the win-dow, sip, and enjoy.

This is the seventh in the Dr. Paul series, coming out at the same time as the third book in the Dog series. What a joy, for me, to have had ten years with such creatures, animal and human!

Mary F. Kohnke

web site: *marykohnke.com*
e-mail: *mfkohnke@mac.com*

Characters in the Book

Dr. Mary Paul, County Commissioner, retired NYU Professor, conservationist. Settled in Palm Valley Florida on the Intracoastal Water Way on a heavily treed parcel with her dogs. An attractive woman with sharp blue-green-gray eyes that change with her mood from laughing and kind to deadly serious. She is decisive, and generous with her time, but doesn't do lunch.

Arthur Steel, Mary's 'very good' friend and financial advisor. He's a tall man in his fifties, with black hair greying at the temples, sharp cheek bones, laugh lines around kind, alert eyes that can go serious in a flash. He's a brilliant lawyer, financial genius, and connoisseur of fine wines; all talents he puts to good use in his adventures with Mary.

Jeffery Stone, a tall, well-built, handsome man with sun-streaked brown hair. His boyish good looks belied his age in the late thirties. Alert blue eyes filled with laughter that can go cold in an instant. More son than friend to Mary and Arthur. He does consultant work with law enforcement agencies of several countries.

Nancy Bird, an old and close friend of Mary. An artist and a psychotherapist. Taller than Mary, with long graceful arms, strong expressive hands, dark brown shoulder-length hair, and hazel eyes. Stylish, in her late thirties. A very striking woman who lives in NYC and does consulting with other therapists when she isn't painting.

Sue Allen, a friend of Mary's who looks enough like her to be a younger sister. She is lithe and graceful, her eyes are gentle but alert, a practicing psychotherapist and with empath/telepath talents she uses when called on by police in New York. She too lives in NYC and is friends with Nancy and Joan.

Joan Bond, another friend of Mary's from NYC. She's a tall, stunning redhead with green eyes. She is very much in charge of her own life and anyone else who she comes across. She's a practicing psychotherapist and a telepath. She's an author and consultant, and more than matches Nancy in her stylish dress. She is very capable and game for anything.

Oliver Santoni, is head of an international crime syndicate. He's in his fifties, medium height, well built, with a look of quiet power about him. He commands the attention of those in his presence without saying a word.

Elmore Victor, Santoni's chief of staff. He's tall, slim, broad shouldered, well dressed in bespoke. Brown eyes with a look that says he's in charge and not a man to cross.

Romano Vargas, Elmore's assistant. He resembles Elmore but is more suave and elegant. He's multilingual, radiates charm and confidence but with an edge that says be careful. He is utterly loyal to Victor and Santoni.

Thomas Hudson, an old nemesis of Mary Paul. He lives in Ponte Vedra and has had several run-ins with Mary. He works for Santoni, but more as a gofer, than a leader. He has a faulty opinion of his value and often needs reminding of just what it is.

MacKenzie Bodega, previous owner of Bodega Vineyards. He sold the property to Mary but has agreed to stay on to help oversee the operation of the vineyards with Sister.

Jack and **Betty Foster,** manager and his wife of Twisted Hills, the first vineyard Mary and Arthur bought some years ago. It has about 250 acres of grapes. It is located next to Bodega Vineyard.

Manuel and **Luciana Salinas,** manager and his wife of Bodega Vineyard. It has over 500 acres of grapes and many more hundreds of acres of forest and streams.

Sister Lopez, Master of Wines at both vineyards and the general overseer and long-time friend of Bodega and his deceased wife. She's a tall, beautiful woman in her fifties with mocha latte coloring. She controls the wine tasting rooms and is a major but quiet figure in the female community of Sonoma.

Don Galeano, head of the Spanish crime syndicate and father of the deceased Pablo Galeano.

Diego Galeano, Don Galeano's son and brother of the late Pablo Galeano

Cesar Ruiz, Pablo Galeano's agent broker in California.

Duchess, Duke, and **Prince,** Mary's German Shepherd dogs.

Sheriff Hall, the Sheriff in Santa Rosa, California.

Sheriff Steve Gray, the sheriff in St. Johns County, Florida.

Chapter One

Sally Day, Mary's housekeeper, came walking down the drive, carrying two glasses of tea. Mary was wearing jeans, a denim shirt and tennis shoes. She was still tan from the summer. Her hair was streaked blond from the sun. She had sharp blue-green eyes that changed with her mood from bright blue when she laughed to green when she wasn't as happy. A very attractive women of middle height, who was aging very gracefully. "Mary," Sally said, "It's time for a break. You've been out here putting the lights and trees up for three hours. You're almost done. Look, you even have the ponds done."

"Yes," Mary replied. She took a glass and sat on the edge of the cart. "It goes fast when you have everything ready. I like starting down there by the road," she nodded her head toward the gates, "and work my way back toward the waterfront. It's such a lovely day. The weather man said by Monday it'll get cold. I hate the cold. You don't think I'm strange putting these Christmas lights up the second week of November, do you?"

"Would it matter?"

"Nope, I'd do it anyhow. I just need some affirmation."

"Nonsense. Since when do you need to be told that what you're doing is okay?"

Mary sat there quietly and thought about that. The Shepherds came and rubbed on her, and she absently petted them. Finally, looking at Sally, she sheepishly smiled. "It's this damn job. Some days it seems like I can't do anything right. I'm not feeling sorry for myself, you hear? Some days, I just feel chipped away at."

"Let me tell you, Mary, I read all the news papers and what they say about you. Surely you knew, when you became the Commissioner, that on every issue half the people would be against it. Multiply that times each issue and it won't take long to piss them all off."

Mary started to speak and Sally shook her arm, "Further, don't forget you live in Ponte Vedra, even if you claim that Palm Valley isn't really part of it. These people aren't used to having anyone tell them no."

Mary laughed, "Especially someone from Palm Valley."

"There you go. I forgot to ask you, are you going to be here for Christmas?"

"No, I'm going back to Sonoma and the vineyards. I promised I'd be back for Christmas week, but I'll be here till then. Arthur will be here for Thanksgiving and the boat parade. I don't know who else. You'll come for Thanksgiving and the boat parade, won't you?" Mary asked as she pulled the cart toward the house.

Sally was quiet as they walked.

"Well?"

"My sister and her husband will be in town."

"So bring them." She stopped. "Unless you don't want them to come."

"It's not that, I just don't want to impose."

Mary walked on thinking. Impose! Lord I haven't heard that word in years. Sally was strong minded and decisive, some times more friend then employee. But she kept what she would call a respectful distance between the two.

"Let me put it this way. I'll need help, as you know, for the boat parade. You and your husband helped last year. I don't know who is coming for Thanksgiving. If it's just Arthur and me I'll be okay. If not, I may need help. Either way, will you come? And if your sister is here, would she consider coming too?"

Sally thought about that. "Fine. We'll come and help, but you aren't paying us. The men can go fish off the dock. Yes, yes," she said as she nodded her head. "That will work just fine. My husband will help with the boat parade too. Parking the cars like last year." She nodded her head again. "Do you want me to help with the rest of the trees and the lights?"

"No thank you. I only have this tree by the bulkhead and one on the dock. Go home! I'll see you next week. I look forward to a quiet weekend of reading."

A few hours later Mary had just poured her late-afternoon glass of wine when the phone rang. Checking the caller ID she smiled, "Hi Arthur, your day almost over?"

"Yes, a long day and an even longer week. How was your week?" All he heard was silence. "Well, surely you have something to say."

"Okay, I just finished putting out all the Christmas trees and lights. It was such a lovely day. The weather people say it will be cold tomorrow."

"Lordy Mary, are we reduced to talking about the weather now? What aren't you saying?"

"I don't like this job. I'm sorry I ran for office. It was much more fun sitting on the outside and telling everyone what they should do and then complaining when they didn't do what I wanted."

Mary heard laughter, deep male laughter that told her how much she was appreciated and loved. There was a difference in being laughed at with love. She even smiled at herself, finally admitting what had been nagging at her all day, and for several days.

"Sally just left. I asked her if she and her husband would be coming to Thanksgiving dinner and the boat parade. She was silent for a while and then said her sister and husband would be in town and she didn't want to impose. Arthur, I was so surprised that she would use a word like imposed with me. I recovered and said I could use her help if she were free. She then made it clear that they would come but I couldn't pay them."

"May I comment?"

"Of course."

"Mary, you are Sally's employer, just like Barbara James was. Barbara was a lovely intimate women like you. She did not talk down to people. But, Sally knew who was boss and where that line was. When Barbara died and Sally came to work for you that relationship was the same. Sally can never assume anything different and you mustn't confuse her by trying to change that."

"Arthur, Barbara had servants all her life, I never had. It seems so strange to keep what seems like an artificial distance."

"Look at it this way. You are only doing what makes Sally comfortable."

"I didn't have any trouble at the Vineyards."

'No, but your relationship with Sally is more intimate than it is with the men who do the yards, clean the barns, pick the grapes…"

"Stop! I got it. Now you are coming for Thanksgiving?"

"Yes, and Jeffery is too. He's just coming in the door. I'll put you on the speaker phone."

"Hi Jeffery."

"Hi Mary. Is Arthur telling you I'll be there for Thanksgiving?"

"Yes, will you ask Nancy?"

"I asked her, she wants to come for the boat parade and can't do both. You also asked her to come to Sonoma for Christmas. She said she can't do them all and be away so often. Also she, Joan, and Babs have charity obligations for Thanksgiving."

"Good, I'll suffer with you guys. We can play golf and if it's warm maybe fish."

She heard them whispering and waited quietly. Finally Arthur started. "Mary, Jeffery has a gadget he wants to connect to my phone, so just wait a minute, please. Don't hang up if it seems the phone has gone dead."

Mary waited and quietly watched a few boats chug north. "Okay, we're back. We've secured this phone so it can't be tapped. Jeffery and I want to talk a bit about what happened in August when Pablo was killed. I've been talking with Santoni about our trip to Europe to look at vineyards. He has also been talking with Jeffery about preventing any fallout from Pablo's father or any of the family, even if we won't be in Spain,"

"Yes, I was wondering about that but it didn't seem I should ask."

"I appreciate that, as does Jeffery. We've made sure there is no record that Hudson, who works for Santoni and was in Sonoma with Pablo, was the person who shot him. There is no coverup. It merely was noted that this man, Pablo, apparently tried to shoot Santoni, due to a misunderstanding on Pablo's part, that Santoni was going to cheat him out of some vineyards.

"Another man was present, who shot Pablo just as he was ready to kill Santoni. This is what Santoni told Pablo's father. He also talked with Jeffery and the Sheriff's of both Napa and Sonoma as well as Mac. As you know Pablo's father heads the crime syndicate in Spain. The same day Pablo tried to kill Santoni and Arthur, his father had arrived in California for the syndicate's international meeting. Spanish officials contacted the father, just after he arrived. They told him they were looking for his son to arrest him and take him back to Spain to stand trial for trafficking in women and children.

"No names of other people who may have been present are in the record. Santoni made it quite clear it would be in everyone's interest if this story could be told. Vendettas were not uncommon among old-world families. Apparently Pablo has been showing signs of irrationality over the past few months, just not in the presence of his father. When Santoni talked with the father, who is an old friend, he told Santoni some of his men tried to tell him about Pablo but he put them off."

"Has everyone been told what you are telling me?"

"Yes," replied Arthur. "I told Sister and Mac. Sister told her niece, Toni. Jeffery stopped in New York. At lunch with Sue, Nancy and Joan, he brought them up to date."

"Jeffery, how are you with all this?" asked Mary.

"I have mixed feelings about Santoni, as you know. I mean, for God's sake, he heads an international crime syndicate. However, I can't help but admire the way the man is taking care of everyone. Himself too, I might add. He has talked at length with Hudson. I believe Hudson is happy to be alive. Have you see or heard from him?"

"No." She laughed. "I think he is very careful to avoid being anywhere I might be. I want you both to know I miss the vineyards, the people, the horses and everything. Further, I can't wait till Christmas. Arthur, did you tell Sister and Mac I was coming home for Christmas?"

There was silence. Finally Arthur said, "Home?"

"Yes, we talked about this, remember, many loves and many homes, so there. While we're on the subject of Christmas, you know I asked Joan, Babs, and Nancy to come to the vineyards for Christmas. Will you make the plane available to them, Arthur?"

"Yes, my dear, I'm at your service. Also I might be able to get them to fly down for two days for the boat parade. If I provide door-to-door service."

"Good. You have always been after me to stop being so frugal and use what I have. What nicer way than for my friends?"

"Mary, I have to run. I'll see you in a couple of weeks."

"Okay Jeffery. Be careful."

"Arthur, is he gone?"

"Yes."

"Tell me, how is he really taking all this about Santoni?"

"Honey, I think he is fine. His main concern is you and me, and now the ladies. He's well aware that we are Santoni's top priority as well. That impresses him. As far as his freelance investigative work is concerned, I don't think he will take on anything that puts him in direct conflict with Santoni or his men, Elmore and Romano. Nor will he do anything to set them up because of his relationship with them. It's new mindset for him. May take a bit to adjust his moral compass. Remember we are not in business with them. We met them way outside of their business. If Jeffery's friends hadn't told us who they were we would never have known and not been the worse for it.

"Mac, Sister and I going to Europe. Santoni will help smooth the way in France and Portugal. The same way you or I would, with people we know and like. That will stretch Jeffery's guardian instinct a bit. I wouldn't be surprised if he shows up over there. But, then he will be leaving you alone in Florida. Some days I think he hopes he could corral us all in one place."

"He had that this summer and look what happened." Mary chuckled. "For a man with no family except an adoptive relationship with you, he certainly has gathered a large extended family."

"Yes, and one he loves and is very protective of. This is so good for him. All he ever had was me and his man-of-steel persona. He never felt vulnerable. He could go around and save the world without any personal attachments, until you came into our lives, dragging all your loving friends along. Think of it, how can he ever manage all of us?" He chuckled.

"Those three in New York are wonderful therapists. They'll help him. Add Sister, another mother figure, he'll do well. I almost forgot, his relationship with Nancy is growing warmer each day. Yes, he's surrounded, I like it. I think he does too, he just needs time for it to jell."

"Do you want to tell me how things are there?"

"No. You tell me how the wine making is progressing. I missed all that picking and pressing and stuff. The more you fill my mind with those lovely activities the happier I'll be and all other things will just float away."

Chapter 2

London

Santoni's secretary looked up at the two men approaching her desk. She smiled. "You two look chipper. Have a good lunch?"

"Yes, thank you Ms. Abbott. The boss said he wanted to see us after lunch. Is this a good time?" Elmore asked with a smile.

"I'll ring and ask him—Mr. Santoni, Mr. Vargas, and Mr. Victor are here." She paused listened, hung up the phone and waved her hand toward Santoni's door.

Santoni waved them to chairs and continued working for a moment. Romano loved the office. It mirrored the man's personality as well as his looks: he had dark hair, beautifully cut, sharp alert eyes and he just looked rich, as did the room. The man, medium in height, solidly built, radiated a sense of power. The room was large, expansive, yet toned down and tastefully furnished. The floor was covered with oriental carpets, mahogany book cases, and easy chairs in a sitting area facing the large windows overlooking the Victoria Embankment and the Thames.

He had asked Elmore once who had done the room. Elmore laughingly told him, Santoni of course, he is very particular what he surrounds himself with, in furnishing as in people.

Elmore was Santoni's chief of staff. He was tall and slim with broad shoulders, dressed in bespoke. He had brown eyes with a look that said he was in charge and not a man to cross. Romano was Elmore's assistant, built like him but more suave and elegant. He had snapping black eyes and radiated charm and confidence. He was multilingual and utterly loyal to Santoni and Elmore.

Santoni looked up. "Elmore, have all the business proposals that were discussed at the California meetings been handled?"

"Almost, sir. My secretary is just finishing the report for you."

"Almost?"

"Trafficking with young girls and children may still be a

problem?"

Santoni put down his pen and stared at Elmore. "Are you suggesting anyone in the consortium is involved or wants to become involved?"

"No, none in the leadership group. However, some of those they deal with, on the fringes of their operations, have dabbled in it. Like Pablo Galeano and his sorry selection of late-night friends. They like the product and like playing with the girls before sending them on, even the children."

Santoni, frowning, shook his head. "Pablo's father called me. He said his men have cleaned that mess up. He asked them to spread throughout Spain and rid the country of them." Santoni paused. "His father hinted that the local federals are turning a blind eye to the cleansing. He's spoken with some of the other leaders and they are making similar efforts. It's easier for him. Spain, a country run by what some called a dictatorship under the guise of royalty, now calling itself a young democracy. The old families and loyalties die hard."

"Sir, I think we have made our position known to others we deal with. They are quietly checking deeper in their territories to see if there is any trafficking. The general public may not like drugs and the rest, but I know they will find trafficking in very young women and children abhorrent. That alone will stir up hornet nests and we will get dragged into it." Santoni stood up and walked over to the windows and stared out. "It seems strange to be on the side of the angels. You know these trafficking people make running guns and drugs and laundering money seem normal. I never felt pure but this other business is filthy. I will do my best to avoid it and help to stop it. So you continue to push them in the same direction.

"I spoke with Mac. All the papers are signed and filed on both properties in California. I have copies of them for you there on the corner of my desk," he said as he waved his hand. Elmore picked up both envelopes and handed Romano his.

"Mac has someone coming in to maintain both my house and yours. He said we might want give some thought to putting the oversight in Sister's hands, as well as talk to the people we bought from and see if they have any suggestions for using the land. I know we have hundreds of acres and we are setting in motion the papers to put it into conservation. We can still farm it any way we want—you know, for cattle or crops. Sister mentioned that she and Mac's late wife looked it over for grapes and for a horse breeding farm. Do you have plans for Christmas?"

"No." They said in unison.

"Would you both like to take the plane and go spend the holidays there and come back after New Year's?"

The men remained silent but were grinning like kids. "I guess the answer is yes." Santoni said smiling. "Mac also reminded me that he, Arthur and Sister will be coming over in early February to visit a few vineyards in France and Portugal. Have you given any thought to which ones would be best for them and who will go with them?"

Elmore said, "Yes, we have a few in mind. Two in France and two in Portugal. We have one more in each if needed."

"Why only two each?"

"Well, we know the men who own each vineyard and they are delighted to have fellow vintners come and especially if accompanied by a Master. Also our friends are Americans and not seen as major competitors. You know Mr. Santoni, these old men and families still look down on the Americans, especially those in the wine business. Very young, they say. Very green. When they taste their wines they just laugh. It is getting better as the American wines mature. Now they sort of smile and say not too bad."

"Good, be sure that Mac and Arthur bring a few cases of their reserve along. Both the reds and the whites. However tell them not to open them till the visit is over. Wouldn't want to divest these men of their prejudice too soon."

"I agree," Elmore said. "It will be worse in France. I thought I would accompany them in France. Romano, will go to Portugal. He is fluent in Portuguese. Me, not so much."

Romano laughed. "I tell him he must learn. If he goes to Brazil he will never find the right kind of girl. However, I am very pleased to go to Portugal. I love Ports. It will be a great learning experience for me. Sister will ask so many of the right questions. Things I would never know to ask. I do so admire her."

"Yes, all those women are admirable. Each in their own way. It reminds me of the old adage that likes attract. I especially liked and admired Mary Paul. She is a wonderful match for Arthur. Will they bring Jeffery along?" Santoni asked.

"I doubt it. He does work, even if freelance. I don't see any ne-farious activity that would attract him to the wine country." Elmore hesitated.

"Well," Santoni said. "You have more to add about Jeffery?"

"Not too much. He is like a wisp of smoke. You catch a glimpse, then it's gone. Makes him a very valuable agent. Especially if he has no known attachment. I would not want him after me."

"Do you have any reason to think he might be?"

"No, Sir. Still, when he first met us he was very watchful. I know he knew who we were. Then when his friends joined all of us at din-ner, I had no doubt."

"Really?" Said Santoni. "Couldn't they just be protective of Mary and her friends?"

"Yes, but to the point that they were all carrying?"

Romano laughed. "I almost had a heart attack when Nancy was sassing Pablo and then leaned forward across the table blocking Pab-lo's view of one of Jeffery's friends, Bob. Bob was sitting next to her. He slipped his gun out of his pocket and dropped it in his lap in one quick motion. She'd leaned forward deliberately, she knew he had a gun."

Santoni laughed. "I told you those women were admirable. El-more, I know what Jeffery does for a living. I asked him before din-ner what business he and his friends were in. He said they were all once in the service of their country. He said he jumped ship before they asked him too, and now he did free lance work but his friends still serve. He said they had some free time and came out to help him set up a new security system at the vineyards. Then they all started to rag on him about being a slave driver, and they all got into it and on each other. It was quite telling about the humor and comradely between them. Admirable men, of a kind I would want on my side in a fight."

Elmore looked closely at Santoni, "You're saying they just hap-pened to all be there at one time? Funny coincidence with the syndi-cate setting up for a national meeting not far away."

"Yes, isn't it. Still, Elmore I couldn't very well ask them if they were here to watch us, now could I?" He smiled. "What amuses me the most, is I'm sure Arthur and Mary knew what those men were there for, beside taking time to help Jeffery with a security system. Can you imagine how they felt when they discovered who we were?"

Romano looked at Elmore and then Santoni. "I'm sorry Sir. You're saying they knew who we were. How did you know that and for how long?"

"I think on a Thursday after the wine tasting at Twisted Hills, after the car attack on Mary, I believe it was. You asked me if you and Elmore could go to Bodega Vineyards and ride with Sister. That Arthur had asked you to come. Then Pablo and Hudson showed up. Didn't you all think that was a coincidence?" He watched Elmore and Romano look at each other. "Well."

Elmore finally said. "You knew when Jeffery told you they had set up a security system."

He paused. "I bet it was a face recognition system. You told me last summer that such things were being developed. If Jeffery and his friends were playing with it, they could have picked us up and who knows who else."

"Yes, and told Arthur and Mary who we were. Arthur's first priority is Mary's safety and he wanted you and Romano there because he knew Hudson and Pablo were unsavory."

"God, I feel foolish and stupid. How could all this have slipped past me?" Romano said, shaking his head."

"Romano, Elmore, do not berate yourselves. You were in the middle of it, I was outside watching. Mac and Arthur are fine men and do not condemn others quickly. Neither, I believe, does Mary. I might add, women are more understanding and able to remove themselves, take a long view."

"You never mentioned any of this to us. Were you going to?" Elmore looked a bit sad.

"Yes, when the time was right. We have been on a pressure-packed few months it's only now getting a bit easier. Do not berate yourself Elmore. You and Romano have been deluged with syndicate business that must come first. Those papers arrived today and brought it all back to me. I thought it time I filled you in on my thoughts.

"You may want to contact Mac and tell him when you will be arriving and how long you will be there. Maybe he will have a rental for you at the airport. I believe there is at least one jeep at the farm. He can put you with the old owners and they will be the best people to discuss the future use of the land. Do not hesitate to ask Sister's advice. You will have fun. Don't forget it's the holidays. I don't know who all will be at Bodega, I'm sure Sister will invite you to ride.

"Still, it would be prudent to call Arthur before you call Sister. Mary is the owner but Arthur in her main person. I don't know where Mary is, probably in Florida. So deal with Arthur."

"Mr. Santoni, will you be spending the holidays here?" Romano asked.

"Yes, I'll mind the store. My family loves the holidays. It is one party after another mixed with shopping. High season for the theater and opera. You name it they will find it. Things are still very unsettled on the continent. You know our people are watching everyone. No one wants to be tainted by the traffickers. The whole mess has drawn unwanted attention—more than usual—to all of us

"The late, very careless and ignorant Pablo has triggered all this. I also fear one of his brothers may have been closer to Pablo than his father realizes. We're keeping a close watch there. The younger brother babbles about needing to find who killed Pablo. We'll wait if anything happens. You can be sure it will be stomped on in a hurry.

"We still have Hudson under close scrutiny. He is working from home and staying very quiet. His computer and phone are open to us. We also have eyes and ears in his house."

"Do you think he knows?" Elmore asked.

"I think he is still scared to death. We'll keep him that way?"

"What about Dr. Mary Paul?"

Santoni laughed. "My secretary keeps an eye on their local newspapers. She's been making changes and taking guff for it. She gives out as much as she takes." He told them about her remarks concerning the old Ponte Vedra people being a 'dysfunctional family' and a few other prize statements.

"Do you think she will last out the next three years of her term?" Elmore asked.

"Oh, yes. Arthur told me she never took vacations her first year.

Last summer was the longest she'd ever been gone. I'll bet that changes."

"I'll tell you, Mr. Santoni I can't see how anyone could stay away. The vineyards are wonderful and the horses and the people are equally as exceptional. I look forward to the holidays."

Chapter 3

Mid December
Friday afternoon

"I'm sure glad Thanksgiving and the Boat Parade are over. Much as I love them, the older I get the more tiresome they seem to me," Mary said on the phone with Arthur.

"You didn't seem tired at Thanksgiving. Was that because it was only family? No need to put on a public face," replied Arthur.

Mary was quiet, finally she said, "You know, I think you're right. The boat parade was sprinkled with, what do we call them, constituents?"

"Mary, in years past they were better known as friends and others who were on the same side."

"Okay, but you saw that bunch. Could you divide them out? The friends from those, what shall I call them…"

"Stop, don't say it. I get the message. Still, it was a big success. Great food, wonderful wine and the boats were especially good. I'm also greatly entertained with your ability to send them home after the last boat passes."

"Oh, Arthur, I've done that for years. I notice who eats, who drinks, and how much. I'm not going to be guilty of sending those poor souls into the dark with more drink than they can handle. Most of the people who have these parties on the waterfront have people staying on at least a couple hours longer. Anyhow, you know I abhor drunks."

"You're careful not to invite them."

"True," she replied, "but sometimes someone slips by."

"Tell me about our final Christmas travel plans."

"As you know Christmas is on a Tuesday. Therefore New Year's is as well. So that lets us off the hook for Mondays. Two full weeks and then some, without Board meetings, so I'm out of here. I think if you come on the Friday of the week before I won't plan to come back till the Saturday after New Years. That's over 15 or 16 days."

"Won't you be missed?"

"Arthur, I'm not going to do what I did this past summer and angle for the time away. It seemed like begging. I'm just going to assume no one will expect me to be around over the holidays and certainly not in the office. I'll have my phone on call forwarding and tell my secretary where she can reach me.

"Which reminds me, Joan said she'll have to be in San Francisco early in the week before Christmas to go over her new book with the publishers. She asked, would I mind if she came to the vineyard early? I told her of course not but to call Sister."

"Yes, Sister called me, she didn't want to say yes and then have me be surprised. You know, if you say someone can stay there you don't need anyone permission."

"I know that, but Bodega is her and Mac's responsibility, it seems it would be rather rude of me to just have people drop in on them without warning."

"Sister sounded delighted that Joan was coming. She even said she probably would make plans to drive to the city and do some last-minute shopping with her."

"Better them than me. Putting them together last summer to do my shopping was a blessing. The last week we were there, after the mess with Pablo, Joan joined us riding. I was surprised how good she was. Sue told me Joan's family has had her in a saddle since she was a tot. She and Sister were a real sight. Can you image them on the town in the city? By the way what are we buying the Fosters and Salinases and their children? Oh my, and Sister and Mac."

"That is the next item on my list. I talked about this with Sister. How about some nice jewelry for the wives? Sister can pick out what they would like and I'll get some great dress watches for the men. She gave me a list of stuff for the kids that she checked out with the parents. High on that list is riding britches and proper boots. She said she and the mothers will go to a local outfitter and take care of it. Wrap the stuff put our names on it."

"Oh my."

"Yes, oh my. You ladies really started something last summer. Sister said when the kids get better, she'll take them to a few local riding shows, both the boys and the girls."

"Can you imagine what their parents think?"

"Mary, everyone is delighted. I also hear they can't wait till you come home for Christmas. They are planning a small horse show. Have you shopped for your friends?"

"Yes, Nancy told me what Joan and Sue wanted. I also bought her a wonderful new set of the finest paint brushes in the world. Jeffery picked them out when he was in New York. I still have Sister, Mac, and Toni."

"Not to worry, Mac ordered a new saddle for Sister from both of us."

"And Mac?"

"Sister gave me a list of wines," he laughed "that will set us both back. Also, she will get Toni something from both of us."

"Good that leaves just you and me. The vineyard is the best gift in the world that you could have given me and I can't wait to get back to it. I got Jeffery taken care of. Sally and her husband want to spend some time, here at the house, over the holiday. Her husband has a list of chores he thinks I need done and will also take the Christmas lights down. I have given up telling them they mustn't. I think it makes them feel it's okay to be here if they do stuff."

"I was thinking. You might want to invite them to the vineyard. Tell them what kind of activities go on year-round and let them pick a time. I just bet if Sally finds out about the canning she will jump all over it. That way she will feel useful. Tell them I'll take them out and back in the plane."

"Arthur what a wonderful idea. I can hardly wait to tell them. Now let me run and finish my reading. The dogs and I will see you at the airport."

Monday, the week before Christmas week, Mac and Sister were in the library going over the last-minute needs for the next few weeks. All the Christmas decorations were up. They all went up before Thanksgiving at both Twisted Hills and Bodega. The weeks before the holidays were a big sales times for both the vineyards. The trees in the tasting rooms at both vineyards were trimmed and white lights were on the trees along the drives leading to the tasting rooms When the sun went down it looked like a fairy land. They stayed open till after six on the two tasting days, and on three Saturdays before Christmas.

MacKenzie Bodega was the recent owner of Bodega Vineyard, he sold it to Mary Paul two years after she bought Twisted Hills the vineyard next door. He was asked to stay on in a constancy role. It was his home for many years and he also had a home on the coast looking over the ocean. He was delighted to be free of the total responsibility of the Vineyard but still have a hand in it. He was in his mid sixties, a tall, ruggedly handsome, well-built man, with twinkling eyes and an abundance of grey-white hair.

Sister Lopez was the Master of Wines for both vineyards. She was fifteen years younger and an old friend of Mac's late wife Babs. She owned acreage and a house between the two vineyards that Babs had given her. She was the majordomo of both Vineyards. There were chief vintners for both Vineyards but Sister controlled the tasting rooms, sales and whatever else she wanted. She was tall, of light mocha coloring, and classically handsome. She was well known in the wine world of Masters and an excellent dressage rider. She had been introduced to Mary as the housekeeper and cook, when in fact she was the overseer of the entire operation.

"Sister, I noticed that you got the house tree trimmed, and lights on those around the yard and pool. Babs used to do that. I forgot how much I missed it."

Sister smiled. "I missed it too. Arthur told me Mary puts out little trees from the main drive into her property down to the waterfront. Trimmed only in tiny white lights. He said she told him it kept the winter dark at bay a bit longer. Said she hates the cold and even in Florida near the ocean that far north it can still freeze. That's a wonderful tree you got for the living room. We had to get the ladder out to trim it. Do you like the job we did?"

Mac nodded and smiling said, "Those are our old ornaments you used, plus red cardinals perched around the room and in the tree. Are those the ones Arthur sent you?"

Sister laughed. "He wanted to surprise Mary. I put greenery and ribbons settings in all the rooms and halls and they have birds hiding in them. Clever, our Mary, with those birds. We even put wreaths in the stables and red bows on the fence around the arena.

"Elmore and Romano are flying in on Friday at the small airport just south of us. The same one Arthur is now using. He and Mary will be in Friday as well. I have a car ordered for Elmore and Romano. There's a jeep at the farm that now belongs to them. Jeffery called and he's coming Friday too with Nancy and Sue. Be fun, we'll have a full house here and I'm sure Romano and Elmore will want to ride. The kids will love it when they come."

"Speaking of the kids. The Foster and Salinas boys and some of the girls asked if they could ride with me when I go out, I said yes. They've never ridden in the forest. They all have a million questions about everything. Like what was it like in the old days." He glanced at Sister who hurriedly hide her smile.

Sister quickly stated, "They are all doing very well with their dressage lessons. They want to put on a show for Mary when she comes." Sister stopped and shook her head. "It is turning into a very different place. I'm glad you sold it to her and Arthur."

Mac nodded and picked up one of the books Sister was reading. "*The Grapes of France.* Are you boning up before our trip?"

"Yes, we won't have long to become experts on champagne, then to hurry on to Portugal to learn all they can teach us about Ports. You know, Mac, we have the chardonnay grapes but we will have to either plant or buy both pinot noir and pinot meunier grapes."

"Yes, some of our fellow vintners grow both and they are very good. There are also some smaller growers we should investigate, those that only sell their grapes. We can do that while we search out the best stock we can find and set the land for planting."

"You know Mac, Luciana is the one, who with Babs, found the grower for the chardonnays. I think we should involve her in this project from the start. She knows everyone as does her husband. We will get a more, shall we say, honest picture from the locals."

"Dammit, Sister, my ancestors go back farther than any of these people."

"I know Mac, but you are of a different class. The owner class. They are not going to whisper their secrets to you." He started to protest and Sister patted his arm and told him, "Luciana will feel very important if he lets her go and search for him. Then when it comes to the buying you and Arthur can swoop in, armed with the best information and let the owner charm you into buying his best product."

"My God, that's what you and Babs did."

"Yes, and then Manuel and Jack came and helped pick out the plantings they wanted."

"You could have done that by yourself."

"Yes, but why ruin the fun? The men, they need to feel smart and useful." Mac stared at her. "Present company excluded, of course."

"How is your Portuguese coming? Are you using those records Arthur sent?"

Sister smiled, "Yes, and he enclosed some in French as well. That's easier but I think I'll understand most of what is said. Don't forget Elmore will be with us in France and Romano in Portugal. I'll know enough to ask good questions. You and Arthur are reading up as well?"

"Oh yes. Don't want to appear too backward. You leaving first thing in the morning?"

"Yes, I should be in the city before noon, miss the early rush."

"Where is Joan staying?"

"At the San Francisco Fairmont. Her publisher got her a suite."

"Good enjoy yourself. I'll talk with Luciana and ask her if she will help Arthur and me put together a list of growers we can inspect."

Chapter 4

Tuesday morning

Sister was almost singing as she drove down Highway 101 to San Francisco.

It was after nine and the morning traffic south was moderate. By the time she hit the city it should be over. She thought of the many times she and Babs had made this trip. After Babs died she had to come to the city for wine meetings and other things, it was not pleasant. There were so many memories she hadn't been prepared to deal with.

Today seemed different. She felt herself buoyant and light: happy, she realized. She almost had forgotten what happy felt like. She mused on it. The sadness, like a fog, had started lifting slowly last year when she began working more closely with Arthur. This past summer when Mary and the ladies arrived it was almost gone. The night Sue was playing Babs's piano and Joan came striding across the room and sat down and began to sing Amazing Grace in her beautiful alto, she'd found herself standing behind her adding her soprano.

She and Mac had tears in their eyes when they heard Sue playing. There was Ghost, Babs's cat, stretched out that on that baby grand like she owned it. The three of then sequenced from one song to another. Her tears had stopped and all she felt was a great warmth welling up around her. The fog was gone and it never returned. What felt so hollow was being filled by these wonderful people. Mary's caring and humor, Joan's companionship when shopping for Mary and the others.

The return to teaching dressage to the ladies and the children. Even the horror of the attack on Mary and Pablo's bloody death didn't mar the new and wonderful peace that had returned. Mary returning the use of the pool to the children of the workers. She accused me of making this a whole new home for her. No, she did it, along with Arthur, Jeffery and their wonderful friends.

Now she had two more grown children to care for. Children, San-toni, the head of an international crime syndicate, had given her to look after. Roman and Elmore, beautiful men who rode like angels and treated her like a goddess, and her beautiful niece, Toni, treated like a baby sister. She smiled and said to herself, I'm singing, inside, and with every reason in the world.

When Joan called and told her she was coming to San Francis-co, and if she finished early with her publisher, could she come to Bodega? Joan had laughed with joy. She told Joan she would come get her and maybe they could get in a couple of days of last minute shopping. Then Joan had called Sunday and said the work would wind up with an all-day session on Monday. Said she would check the papers and have a couple or so places lined up for them to shop on Tuesday.

Mary had called, and when Sister told her she would go pick Joan up, Mary asked her if she would mind getting Arthur some dress boots. She gave her his size. She laughed when Mary she told her he needed to look like a native when they went out to dinner and not a Chicago big shot. Susan's sister checked his closet and decided she would get him a western dress belt as well from she and Toni. Then she thought I better check Jeffery's sizes as well just in case. She wanted something for Elmore and Romano. Something smart, horsey and sophisticated. Yes, Joan would be the perfect shopping companion for this.

Sister pulled under the portal at the entrance to the Fairmont, her door opened immediately. "Thank you, I'm Sister Lopez, I'm Dr. Joan Bond's guest." The man looked at his list and smiled, "Of course Ms. Lopez," he looked over at the door, waved, and a man hurried over and took Sister hand as he helped her out of the car. "Welcome Mas-ter! I see I have timed your arrival perfectly."

Sister smiled broadly, "Carlos, how wonderful. What is the finest concierge in the world doing opening doors for a country girl?"

He bent and kissed her hand. "Country girl. No, only for the fin-est Master in the world."

Sister put her hand to her chest, "Oh my, be careful I shall faint with such flattery." She gave him a hug. "It's good to see you."

"It has been too long. Do you have much luggage?" He asked.

"No just an over night and a small garment bag. We hope to leave for Bodega Thursday morning at the latest."

"Will you dine with us tonight?"

"Yes, unless Dr. Bond has other plans. You have met her, Carlos?"

"Not for any conversation, only to admire from a distance, as she strides through the lobby or to a restaurant. She is a strikingly beautiful woman—such power, such grace! Ah, but she is only second to you, Master."

Sister threw back her head and laughed. "Carlos, you bring me such joy," she said as they walked through the lobby.

The elevator doors opened and they heard, "Oh My God! You have again taken the most attractive man in the place." Joan rushed out and laughingly hugged Sister. Carlos stood back and frankly admired these two tall, very handsome women. As did many others in the lobby.

One, a tall stunning redhead with brilliant green eyes. The other equally tall and exceedingly handsome with mocha latte coloring and sharp snapping black eyes.

"I got impatient and thought I'd wait down here for you. Do you want lunch? Do you need a moment to freshen up?"

"No, I haven't been on the road long. Are you ready to shop?"

"I'm always ready to shop."

Sister turned and asked Carlos if someone could put her luggage somewhere and she would get it later. "No, Sister. I will put it in Dr. Bond's suite myself. The Maitre d´ and our Sommelier heard you were coming and look forward to seeing you at dinner tonight. I hope, Dr. Bond, that doesn't interfere with plans you have made."

One of Joan's eyebrows shot up and her mouth twisted into a shrewd half smile. "No, Carlos, is it? I seem to have found myself in the presence of royalty."

Carlos quickly touched and hushed Sister, bowed and said, "Indeed you have. May I chat with you later, Sister?"

"Yes, of course, please come up when we get back. We can catch up." She gave him a quick kiss on the cheek, put her hand around Joan's arm and steered her toward the doors.

Joan grabbed Sister's hand as they exited the hotel. "Oh my, what a wonderful start for my vacation. Lets share our shopping lists. I bet we will find we share some of the same places."

Sister grabbed a cab at the door and mentioned a popular equestrian store. They traded notes on what they were looking for and realized they both wanted things for the men. Sister told Joan the boots were from Mary and got Arthur's dress boots immediately. She then matched them with a beautiful belt and dress buckle from her. Joan suggested a lovely money clip that she could get him; he could easily put it in his riding britches. Then they both laughed and said, why not duplicate these things for Jeffery from them and Toni. Even though Jeffery didn't ride as much, he could still be well dressed, for a westerner.

"Joan, Elmore, and Romano are going to be in for the holidays. Lets get them something from their five lady friends... well, six, if we add Toni."

"Yes, something smart and very sophisticatedly British, but with a horse or something on it," Joan said.

They discussed this with the store manager, who had joined them when the purchases had begun piling up, and he noticed who the ladies were. He went in back and brought out a small box of money clips that he said had just come in. Etched very discretely on the gold surfaces were dressage horses standing on their hind legs. They were different from each other, but all distinctive and beautiful.

Sister and Joan looked at each other and smiled. "Perfect!" they said in unison. Then they looked again and added, "For Mary and Sue too."

"You know," Joan said. "Mary uses a money clip and I can just see Sue flashing this in a smart New York restaurant. I do wish they had one for an artist."

"Madam, what about this one?" The manager held out a thin sterling silver clip with paint brushes crossed over a palette.

Joan eyed the manager, tipped her head, "You do gift wrap and deliver on the same day?"

"Where?"

"The Fairmont."

"They will be there before you finish lunch. Which I might suggest you try the lovely tea shop next door."

Sister smiled, "Good idea, I know it well. I believe your wife is the manager there."

He shyly smiled, "Yes Sister, she is and we have missed you."

They paid and asked that each wrapped package have a small card and name attached that they filled out. After they were settled in a corner booth surround with hanging plants. Joan asked, "Do you know everyone?"

"I visited the city for many years. Alone and with Babs, Mac's wife, before she died."

She looked around. "This was one of our favorite places to catch lunch," she looked down.

Joan reached across the table for her hand, "We don't have to stay here, you know."

Sister looked at her and smiled, "You are so thoughtful. After twenty- something years they would have to move the whole city. I was thinking, shopping with you has been such a joy, and happy new memories best soothe old ones." Then they compared what was left on the must-do list of gifts. They decided one more stop on the way back to the hotel today, and the rest could be done tomorrow.

Late afternoon at Joan's suite. There was a quiet knock at the door. Sister said to Joan, "I'll get it. I think it's Carlos." He came in carrying a tray with three glasses and a small champagne bottle nestled in a silver ice bucket.

"Just a small toast to your return." He smiled and bowed to Sister.

Joan, standing across the room, watched Sister take the tray from him, give him a big hug and a kiss on the cheek. "Now my friend, I know you are sincere but I know this precedes some serious talk. May Joan join us?"

"Yes, if she will not be bored by talk of wine and exams."

"Oh Carlos, you have passed your Masters exams."

"Yes, all but the research paper. I was going to call you. Then I heard you were coming. I couldn't help but seek you out for some advice on a tricky problem. You are not upset?"

"Of course not. Some years ago when you told me you were going to work on the Masters of Wines courses and exams I was thrilled. It is a hard road. You have a Masters in Oenology but the rest is equally as hard. Joan will you join us?"

"Yes, for a sip of what I am sure is a wonderful champagne. When the talk gets too technical for me I will scoot off for a quick shower before dinner."

Not long after, Carlos and Sister were deep into the intricacies of creating the various blends and what makes one better than another. Joan quietly left when the questions turned to whether it was the grape, the soil, the climate, and whatnot. Carlos presented his experiment and what he hoped to produce and his questions. About forty minutes later Carlos clapped his hands, "Yes, yes, of course. That will do it. It is so simple! I never would have gotten it without you."

"No, Carlos. You would have seen it. We just made it come a bit sooner. Your research is original and very clever. I would suggest you copyright your paper before you present. It is not due till June."

"May I add your name as a consultant? I have two others."

"Yes, do that. If a Master has given you a suggestion or two and it's footnoted, it is less likely some will copy your ideas. The Institute is very careful of those who infringe on a new student's research, or on anyone's for that matter."

Joan looked in and Sister waved her over. Soon Carlos left and Sister prepared herself for dinner. "You don't mind eating in the hotel, do you Joan? I mean you've been here all week. You may be tired of it."

"No, I mostly ate here in my room, there was so much I needed to read and approve. I knew if I wanted to get out of here in time to go with you I had better pour it on. You know once you get into the rhythm of the editing and all the changes, it goes better if you stay with it. Thank God the people, my publisher had working with me felt the same. Of course I think they wanted to get out of here before Christmas."

Without consulting each other they both wore black sheath thigh-length evening dresses. They were stunning and strode out of the suite arm in arm. The Maitre d' looked at them and bowed, everyone in the dining area turned and watched them as they crossed to a lovely table over looking the city. "That, Sister, was a grand entrance. We have missed you. Dr. Bond you are indeed equally as lovely, a fitting companion to Sister."

"Enough Mark. All the flattery will surely turn my head."

"Why not, it has turned all the heads here tonight. Sister, Elliott, our Sommelier, asks if you will allow him to bring you a wine he is trying out. Just a taste, he says he doesn't want to suggest it to people till he is absolute sure it is perfect."

"Mark I don't believe that for a minute. However, I will let you two have your fun."

Sister, Joan and Mark discussed the menu. They settled on the rack of lamb with asparagus tips and Mark suggested a small salad medley. Elliott, the Sommelier, came to the table. He had four glasses in one hand and a bottle wrapped in a white napkin in the other. He set the glasses down. He had pulled the cork previously, he poured an inch into a glass and handed it to Sister.

She carefully held it up to the candle light and admired the lovely deep red color. She swilled it in the glass and took a deep smell. Raising her eyes she looked at Elliot, "Hum, I don't believe this." She took a sip and swilled it around in her mouth, rolled her eyes, swallowed and sighed.

"It is a 1957 Cab Reserve from the Bodega vineyard. At today's prices, at least $500 or more a bottle. How ever did you get your hands on it?"

Elliott laughed, "I told you she would recognize it."

Mark smiled, "May I taste?"

"Elliott, please sit and pour for each of us. Joan, I hope you like it. It's rare to find one that is not lodged deep in our caves. How did you find it?"

"Mrs. Bodega always kept some here in our vaults. We kept them to age and just couldn't bring ourselves to offer them to just anyone. You are not just anyone." They all sipped and sighed.

Sister teared a bit and smiled. "Thank you. What a wonderful welcome back."

Chapter 5

J oan and Sister were sitting in the suite's living room. They indeed spent the day on the town. They had their feet on the coffee table sipping a port for an after dinner drink. They'd had a quiet dinner in the suite after the rigorous exercise, they called shopping. "I don't think I can move, and if you promise not to tell anyone, I'm shopped out."

"Joan, I would love to have that on tape for our friends, but since I'm in full agreement, I promise I'll never tell. That very late lunch saved me. I think I have everything I need and then some. It will be a very good Christmas. I am so very happy."

Joan watched her carefully and gently said, "How long has it been, since you've been able to say that?"

Sister half smiled. Stood and walked to the windows overlooking the city. "Over two and a half years. About three months before Babs died. She went down suddenly. I thought my life had gone with her. If I hadn't had the vineyards, the Fosters and Salinases and their children and Mac to look after I don't believe I would have made it." She was quiet for a minute. "I was only in my early twenties when Babs took me into her life. She gave me the room Nancy now uses when she's there."

"You don't need to talk about this, you know." Joan quietly said. "I'm not trying to play therapist with you."

Sister smiled, and rejoined her on the couch. "No. I don't think you would. I've not talked to anyone about my life at Bodega. Only bits and pieces to Mary. I was in my early twenties, and Babs was only about ten years older than me, when I arrived there, and she had the two children. At first I helped with them, and learned to run the house. Then I learned the grapes, the vines, the horses, everything. She made me go to college and of course I studied Oenology. Then I got a Masters in Oenology and then began my studies in the institute for my Master of Wines." She paused. "It sounds like a lot, and much work, but, Joan, the time flew. I was very happy. I was in heaven."

"The children, what of them?" Joan asked.

"Babs's parents were from the East. They were very wealthy, had homes in New York City, Boston, and when Babs met Mac and married him, they bought a home here in the City as well. They found it very difficult to accept Babs leaving a successful concert career to live on what they called a farm. They made Babs see doctor after doctor. They couldn't understand her being an empath and what that was doing to her on the stage. Mac understood immediately when she explained it to him. He worshiped her. He saved her life and her sanity.

"The children are both brilliant. The boy's a violinist, a genius, and the girl's a physician—a surgeon. Babs's parents didn't interfere while the children were in elementary school. Then the boy got hold of a violin at school when he was six. Babs found a man nearby to teach him. The girl began skipping grades in school. The grandparents descended and insisted they come live with them in the city and attend private academies here. The children thrived at the city schools. They came home to Bodega, of course, on vacation, some weekends, and holidays. It became obvious they couldn't wait to return to school even though they loved their mother. Mac was distant, not cold, but not a warm loving father. He didn't know how to play with them, and wasn't eager to learn.

"The girl was the oldest, both were precocious. When the boy's teachers suggested he go to the Juilliard School of the Arts, the girl wanted to go to a private school in New York as well. Babs saw the handwriting on the wall and did not object. She told me once, she wanted to raise happy children. She prayed they would not be bedeviled with her psychic gifts.

"Mac, he did whatever Babs wanted. She loved her horses, she made a fine horse woman of me. She loved the vineyards and threw herself into the life here. We traveled to horse shows, won ribbons, and shopped. Joan, she had a full life and made my life equally full. Then my baby sister came to me, beaten almost to death, and delivered Toni before she died. Babs accepted her as a member of the family, as did the Salinases. I guess I could say we all raised each other.

Babs died peacefully and Mac and I have soldiered on. Arthur and Mary bought Twisted Hills about then. Arthur spent time with Mac and me, then they bought Bodega."

Sister looked at Joan and smiled. "So here you and I are, helping to create Christmas for a whole new family. A very large diverse family."

"I'm glad I'm here," Joan said. "I don't have any family left. I have a million colleagues in New York and around the world. Sue is the closest to me now, then Nancy and recently Mary. Being a psychic has a way of distancing oneself from others. Also as a therapist one builds walls. Sue has been such a relief, her sister Babs, who was killed last summer was too. You know Babs was an empath like your Babs. She did therapy with children. She couldn't stand to work with adults. We have a national organization of psychics. We provide a support system for each other."

"How did you get to know Nancy?"

"In New York. She's a superb therapist, especially for psychics and other therapists. She loves her art most, but she conducts seminars that are raved about. We had one with her in St. Augustine. I organized it. That's where Babs was killed. The autopsy showed she had an inoperable brain tumor. One could say it was a blessing. Sue is recovering. I think being here and being with the horses this summer was therapy in itself."

"She looks like Mary. Mother and daughter or older sister," Sister said. "Remarkable."

"Yes, what's more fun is, neither of them recognize it in themselves. Last summer when Babs was still alive, to see the three of them together was a real eye turner. It wasn't until you got close to them that you could see Mary was older. Even in bathing suits Mary looked their age."

"I noticed this summer. It's rare to have so many beautiful women together. I might add men as well," Sister said with a smile.

"Oh la! Wasn't that true? We had fun with that when Elmore and Romano showed up. I thought Jeffery was going to have a fit. Threatened his harem. I over heard Mary straightening him out. You sure he's not her son?"

"Might as well be, he worships her and Arthur."

"And you, Sister."

"Yes, he did a wonderful service for Toni and me. You know, Joan it's easy to love when you're loved. We're able to be demonstrative with each other."

"I saw that when we arrived last summer."

Sister smiled, "Mary was taken by surprise, then it turned into the loveliest of expressions. When I think about it I would describe it as one of deep satisfaction. She seems to find a great deal of peace and satisfaction when the people she loves behave in a loving way with each other. It's like she looks it all over, then walks away and goes about whatever else might be on her mind."

"That's true, Sister. It is not dismissive or cold; you are not ignored. It's like she has placed you, in respect to herself, and no more needs to be said. She certainly is not demonstrative even with Arthur. A quiet touch of the hand or a look. She will listen to him even argue and tease but I've never heard anger. I've watched her reach out and touch someone and curl into a hand that is placed in a loving way on hers," Joan paused. "I like her. I feel respected and liked, period.

"Oh my, I am listening to us. I think this is an interesting way of getting to know each other without being too obvious about it. Is that what we are doing, Sister? A lovely, gentle intimate dance of the minds. Very nice. I like it! I think I am going to have a wonderful Christmas in many ways.

"Now to bed, we are leaving after a good breakfast. You said it will be against the traffic. Will we be home in time for the Thursday tasting?"

"Yes, we will and happily welcomed by the Salinases and Fosters."

"You mean I'm expected to go directly to work?"

"Yes, my love. To work."

London
Wednesday afternoon

"Well, Elmore, Romano are you both ready to leave?" Santoni asked as he waved them into chairs.

"Yes, Mr. Santoni. It seems all of our business colleagues are slowing down over the holidays. We have left word with our secretaries to call us immediately if something comes up that needs our attention. They're not to be bothering you with everyday work product." Then Elmore hesitated, "I got a call from a client in Spain. He said a friend of his ran into the oldest Galeano brother at a party. Said, after quite a few drinks the young man started raving about avenging his brother Pablo's death. That he knew Americans were trying to steal from Pablo. He said when Pablo caught them they killed him."

"Did he name anyone?"

"No, he was heavy into the booze and even drugs. His name is Diego and he was only two years younger than Pablo and apparently he followed him everywhere. Pablo was teaching him the business. Seems he was learning more that the wine business."

Santoni got up from his desk chair and walked to the windows and stared out. "Did he happen to mention anything about the father?"

"No. The only other thing mentioned was the complaining, from some, about the crackdown on the trafficking of girls. It seems the word got out and spread rapidly. If anyone got caught messing in that stuff the syndicate would cut them dead. It is even being said that the Federals will work with the syndicate to stop the trafficking."

Santoni turned and smiled. "They are saying that are they? Good, encourage it. Makes us look good. Well, better. I'm sorry for my friend Galeano. Tough to lose a son but to have a second following in the same path. I can only assume he knows nothing about this. I cannot be the bearer of bad news either. Not after being in the same room when his son was killed. Elmore, tell our people to listen for news and report to you immediately. Also they are to have nothing to do with this young man."

"Yes, sir."

"You are leaving tomorrow?"

"Yes, we will have a stop over in Atlanta. Then on to California. We could do it in one day but that is a long haul. We will take turns piloting and stick to a southern route. The weather can turn bad in a hurry over the middle of the country. Since we are going West the sun will be following us, so we will get in early. Sister will have a car waiting for us."

"Good, Romano. Have you both done your Christmas shopping?"

Romano smiled. "Yes, we both shopped together. Perfume for the ladies and Port for the men. That way we can share their gifts in taste and smell." He raised his eyebrows, "No?"

"Very good." He walked back to his desk and reached into a drawer and took out a smallish white box with gold strips. He took the lid off and pushed it across his desk. Both the men leaned forward and looked at a matte black, almost flat, automatic. It looked like it could slip into your pocket and never be seen.

Elmore said, "May I?" as he reached toward the box.

Santoni said, " No. There are directions to read first." He handed a booklet to Elmore.

"My God, it's not metal, it's that space age stuff. The bullets are the same material. I read about them," he said as he quickly scanned it. "Good. Very simple." He raised his eyebrows, "And I bet very expensive."

"True on all counts." He opened a lower drawer and took out a larger box. "There are six more in here. Two are for you and Romano, Merry Christmas! The other four are for Arthur, Mac, Sister, and Jeffery. This one is for Mary." He slipped it out and when he turned it over it was white.

"Oh my. Depending on what she is wearing it will disappear. Is the one for Sister like that?"

"Yes. We have exposed them all to danger. I want them to have the best we can provide to protect themselves. Sister and Mac will be working for us, having oversight of our property. Arthur and Mary are directly connected with the vineyards. Jeffery is their family.

"When Sister comes to Europe, tell her I want her to carry this everywhere. I'll tell Mac and Arthur. He can tell Jeffery. There are boxes of bullets. Please tell them once they get the feel of the gun. They are to practice their accuracy with their own guns and bullets. These are too expensive to waste. You will also want to tell them, and especially Jeffery, these are not on the market yet, if ever. So I don't think he should try to have them registered. I'm sure he will understand." He gave them a half smile. "I would love to see his face. You will tell me."

Romano asked, "May I?"

Santoni looked at him, then gently nodded and smiled, "Please do."

Romano gently picked up the gun, turned it over in his hand, clicked on the release, and it popped open. He examined the inside and released the cartridge. The bullets emptied into his hand on a hankie. He whipped them off, reloaded them, and closed the gun. He smiled, and then wiped the gun on the hankie in his hand and replace the gun in the box.

"You worked on developing this gun, didn't you, Romano?"

"Yes, sir. One of my many hobbies. I didn't know it was ready for distribution."

Elmore looked at him with raised brows. Romano smiled at him. "One of my father's many sidelines. Although I do not work in the company, he knows my love for guns and brings his pets to me to play with. This was my favorite. It is, how do I say this, not exactly top secret, but almost. His greatest fear and the governments was for it to fall into the hands of terrorists. Criminals not so much, they have families and care for their countries. It is the mad men among us who we all should fear." He smiled at Santoni. "I am delighted he does not consider you among that group."

"No, my young friend. We talked about our trip to Sonoma. He suggested I give these to our new friends." He looked at Elmore, "Don't be troubled, Elmore, I have known Romano's father for many years. When Romano became restless at school and couldn't find a place for himself and happened on you at college, I was only too delighted to add him to the company at your suggestion."

"Sir," said Elmore, "Romano and I have a very small gift for you." He pulled a small box from his pocket and handed it to Santoni. Inside was a platinum key on a platinum key ring. It shone like the sun, in the desk lamp light. On the end was a St. Christopher's medal also in platinum. "It is for the house on the ocean."

Santoni head bowed. Finally, he smiled and looked at his men. He thought to himself, no not his men, sons. "Thank You. Now off with you and don't be late coming home."

Chapter 6

Friday
Airport in Sonoma

"Who will land first?" Joan asked, sitting next to Sister in the seat of the Mercedes at the airport.

Sister laughed. "I'll bet they will be here within a half hour of each other."

"Is that why you had the van from the vineyard come with us?"

"Yes." She looked at Joan. "Think about it. This is a family with all the competitiveness of real siblings, especially the men. The adults are flying in from Florida. They couldn't care less about who gets here when. They know we'll be here waiting for them. Jeffery has made this trip many times. He knows how long it will take them and him. Elmore and Romano are very careful men who plan their lives well. They are also considerate and if there are problems they will want to be here to help."

Joan stared at her. "Does this kind of planning and analysis come naturally or have you worked at it?"

Sister reached over and squeezed Joan's hand. "No, my friend, like you, I have had to study people and figure out what they will do or buy. It's not difficult once you have all the parts and information. Put it together enough and it becomes easy and fits a pattern."

"Okay. Who will land first? Given that the weather doesn't effect them."

"If they have a choice, the boys will. So they can help everyone else with their luggage. Jeffery will be right on top of them, then the elders come leisurely behind and be waited on. As is proper."

Joan sat there quietly and thought about what Sister said. "Also, none of them will want to inconvenience you by making you wait too long or make two trips."

"You got it. See, you'll be a Master someday."

"You don't need to ask or plan, you just have to be considerate and know your people. You know that will be in my next book. It is really very simple. All you need is to know your people and care."

Arthur looked out the window as they taxied to the small hangar office. "Look Mary, we have a welcoming committee."

Mary leaned past him and saw men and women lined up on the tarmac in front of two cars and a van. "Good timing. Wonder who figured that out?"

"Ask Sister. I'll bet she has a clever answer for you."

Just as the steps from the plane hit the ground the three dogs raced out and quickly attended to their business. The males marked the nose wheel of the plane, then raced to Jeffery and Sister. Quietly, they sat and watched Mary and Arthur greet everyone.

Mary gave Sister a hug and gently pulled her to the side and, looking up at her, asked, "Would you mind if we included the boys in our Christmas celebrations?"

Sister looked at her and half smiled. "What did you have in mind?"

"Well, like Christmas Eve dinner, and they can come and ride when it suits you." She looked up at Sister to gauge her response. "Maybe dinner tomorrow night as well?"

Sister could restrain herself no more. She grinned, "I fear Toni beat you to it. She also remembered who owned the vineyards. She asked me to ask you if she could ask them?" "I remember. However, you run the place and two more people can be chosen. I don't want to impose. Well… unnecessarily, that is."

Sister pulled Mary into a hug. "I do love you, Dr. Mary Paul. You are my Christmas present, the Christmas present we all might have hoped for, if we only knew." Before Mary could say more Sister steered her to Elmore and Romano.

Mary recovered rapidly. She put her arms through both of theirs and said, "I want to be sure you understand, this is one big family and you are part of it. So for starters tomorrow, come and ride and eat dinner with us, that is unless you have plans. Also come whenever you want and plan on Christmas Eve and Day." She turned to Sister, "Could I make it any clearer?"

"No dear, you did just fine." She turned to the boys, "The fridge and cupboards are stocked with foods at Santoni's house since you said he wanted you to stay there. We will get together and talk about the future concerning your property tomorrow or whenever you are ready. I have some suggestions and Mac has some people we want you to meet. Is that okay?"

"Yes, Mama," they both said. "We have presents to deliver tomorrow. Will noon be okay?"

"That's fine. Lets load up, Mary. Looks like all the luggage is in the van. We can all fit in the Mercedes station wagon." She got in behind the wheel and Arthur held the front side door open for Mary.

Mary looked around and, turning, asked "Arthur, isn't this like the one we had last summer?"

"The same."

"Same? As in like or same."

"Same. It's one of my Christmas presents to you. To the vineyard actually, but since you own it, it's yours."

Mary continued to look back at him and move her hand in a come-on fashion. "Okay, I contacted the Mercedes rental company and asked what they were going to do with it. They said the insurance paid for most of it and they would sell it for whatever they could get. I called the Sheriff and he got that man who runs a 'shade tree' auto repair business. You know the brother of the man who hit you with his truck. He still felt so bad about this brother's behavior that he told the Sheriff he would fix it like new, if the body was still okay.

"He and the Sheriff went to the Mercedes place and he looked at it and the Sheriff said he did a lot of 'tut tutting' and head shaking. The longer he took the lower the price got, till he looked at the Sheriff and winked. The Sheriff said he would take it. I had given the Sheriff a signed bank draft and he paid on the spot and the mechanic had his truck and hauled it away."

"Why, it was drivable the last I had it!"

"Looked better, the Sheriff said, to see it being hauled away."

"For just scratches."

"Mary, Mercedes don't have scratches."

"Oh, God."

Sister laughed. "Bandits, this family is full of bandits. Mary, I took it to San Francisco to get Joan and it drives like a dream and holds so much room for packages."

"You go, girl," said Joan. "Why, we could've even gotten more."

Sister coughed. "Well, more if we had a few more days," Joan added.

Arthur jumped in, "I had a phone put in and a camera like the cop cars have. You have to play with it, Jeffery..." and off the conversations went in many directions; everyone playing catch up.

"Sister, will Toni come and have dinner with us tonight?"

"She's home now, helping with the preparations I think we can ask her to stay," she said with a quirk to her lips. Then she turned toward Mary, "Be hard to keep her away, I'm afraid."

"Don't! I want you both around as much as you can stand it. Further, I don't want to have to keep repeating myself. This is your home as much as mine. Period." They were soon turning into the drive and even if it wasn't quite dark, you could see all the lights on the trees all the way up to the house, down to the stables and tasting rooms and everywhere.

Mary's eyes were big and she just stared, Sister looked over and saw the sheen on her eyes, and reached and squeezed Mary's hand and whispered, "Merry Christmas."

Everyone in the car was quiet and staring just like Mary. Babs's eyes were teared up like Mary's. Joan and Nancy had their arms around her shoulders. Babs whispered, "I'm so glad I came. You all are making it so much easier. I was so afraid of this first Christmas alone."

"You are not alone, honey." Nancy murmured, "And I bet Ghost is waiting as well."

Sister heard her and said, "She is that."

After unpacking, Mary went down to the living room with her arms filled with presents. There was a huge tree near one set of French doors that opened onto the pool deck. It had already acquired many packages, brightly wrapped and ribboned. She put hers under the tree and looked at the red birds perched in the tree with the bulbs. She then walked around the rooms and noticed the green foliage setting, each with a red bird hidden inside it. She smiled and thought of Arthur. She knew he had told Sister and probably sent her the birds. What a lovely man.

It had been a mild day when they arrived, about 60 degrees. Sister told her it would drop in the evening. She noticed that the fireplace had already been laid, waiting for someone to set a match to it. She moved to the library and the fireplace there was laid as well. She sat in a deep Queen Anne chair in front of it and put her feet on an ottoman and leaned her head back, thinking, what peace, and dozed off.

Later, Toni came in and was about to ask Sister if she wanted her to light the fire. She looked at Mary, then Sister. Sister put her finger to her lips and whispered to Toni, "I'll light this one, you get the one in the living room."

She bent and worked on the fire then put the screen back, sat back on her heels and gazed at it. She heard, "Cozy, yes. You work on cozy."

She turned her head. "Ears like a cat, have you?"

Mary put her feet to the side and patted the ottoman. Sister sat and smiled. Mary said, "I don't know how you could have made things any nicer. It looks like a wonderland. Did you decorate the horses?"

"Tomorrow, want to help?"

"Bows, ribbons and maybe even bells?"

"On the horses or the riders?"

Mary smiled and reached for Sister's hand. "I've missed you; and speaking of missing..." she looked as all three dogs quietly came in and lay near them. "Waiting for dinner. I think they followed you."

"There they are. Did they wake you? They heard. Do you like everything? Is everything okay for you?" babbled Toni as she looked around.

"With a squeeze to Sister's hand, Mary reached out to Toni's. "It is better than lovely. I couldn't be happier."

Toni lit up. "Good! We did everything Arthur asked, and then some of..." She looked at Sister. "Oops, I shouldn't have said that. I guess."

"Toni, it's fine. I had no trouble seeing Arthur's fine hand at play but you and Sister made it work."

"Oh thank you."

"There you all are." Nancy said coming in the door with a tray of hors d'oeuvres and glasses. "What are we drinking Master?"

"Hum," Sister said. "A Chardonnay for Babs. Merlot for Mary and a bottle of Cab for all who don't want the other. I'll get it."

"No, my dear, don't get up. I have them," Mac said as he came through the door, his hands filled with wine bottles, soon followed by the others.

Chapter 7

Barcelona, Spain,
December

Galeano was in his city home working in his office. It had been a busy Fall. He had finally put the pain of his son Pablo's death behind him. He was relieved that it was finally over. He told his friend Oliver Santoni he had no knowledge of his sons various misbehaviors. That was not precisely true. His men told him of Pablo's drinking and occasional drug use. His misbehavior with women finally came to his attention when Pablo got a local girl pregnant. It was the daughter of one of his best vintners.

The vintner's second oldest daughter had been acting very upset and finally his wife had gotten the truth out of her. The girl told her father that Pablo had raped her. She said Pablo told her if she told her father he would have him fired and driven out of the country. The mother sent her to her sisters far from their home. Then she told her husband he must talk to Galeano because Pablo threatened to get her younger sister next.

The vintner came to Galeano, twisting his cap in his hands. He said he must move on to another vineyard far away. Galeano finally got the truth from the man. He was so sick he could hardly keep himself from beating his son half to death. He told his vintner he was not to move; that his son would not come near him or any of his family ever again.

He'd called Pablo to come to Barcelona to talk with him. They owned several vineyards and his son had oversight of two of them plus he was also getting involved in the syndicate business. He thought he was doing well till this happened. When Pablo came in, he did not hesitate to tell him he knew what he had done. He also said he was never to go to that vineyard again. He would have his vintner manage it and he would do the oversight.

He went on to make it clear what he thought of his disgraceful behavior. He told him if he ever found him engaging in anything like that again he would write him out of his life. His son turned white. It was obvious that he didn't think his father would react so seriously. He knew how his father ran his business and believed he would do what he said. That was three years ago. He'd had his men watch him closely for some time, apparently not long enough.

When he got back to Spain with Pablo in a coffin. He had a quiet burial at the family home. His wife, the sisters, and three other brothers were very sad. After the burial he decided to tell the rest of the family the truth. He told them the authorities had contacted him as he was leaving for America, that they had extradition orders to find Pablo and bring him back to Spain to stand trial, and why.

He said he had been told Pablo had been acting strangely and drugging. That he was heavily into trafficking in young woman and children. He told them Pablo threatened the owners of vineyards in Sonoma, and his friend Santoni. That he was holding a gun on both the vineyard owner and Santoni. He was ready to shoot him when another man shot Pablo before he could pull the trigger.

He looked out the window. It had been very hard on all of them. Two of the younger brothers and sisters seemed less surprised. Later, his wife told him Pablo had been bullying them. However, the next oldest son, Diego, was very upset. He spent more time with Pablo and was learning the business from him. He said he never saw Pablo behaving badly, never saw him take drugs, nor did he see him with young girls.

Galeano had contacted his men and sent them out after the men Pablo had been running around with and doing the business of selling girls. He told them to let them think they were interested in taking up where Pablo has left off. They could even insinuate that the big boss might like a share. They were to tape and record everything.

After he saw and read it all, he got hold of a Federal he knew and told him what he found and that he would eliminate the men Pablo dealt with directly and expected the Federals to get rid of the rest in Spain.

He told his son, Diego, what he had found and showed him the evidence. He also reminded him Pablo had almost killed his friend Santoni, the head of the syndicate. Diego had cried and yelled and said maybe that was so, however, he knew Pablo had been murdered by people in America. Americans, not Santoni. Americans, who wanted Pablo's money. He had stormed out of his office.

God, Galeano thought, as he continued to pace the floor, looking out the widow. Do I need to have Diego watched as well? Was Diego into drugs? Was that why he was acting so crazy? He rang for his senior staff man, Mateo, the same man who had taken care of getting rid of Pablo's unsavory friends.

When he came, he told Mateo what was going on with Diego. What his son said. He said he was afraid his son would try to find a way to avenge Pablo. He paused and looked at Mateo. "Have you heard anything?"

Mateo was not afraid of anyone or anything. He had been Galeano's enforcer for years. He had once told him about Pablo's behavior, and his father had dealt with it. He suspected Pablo was into many other things but he had no evidence before Pablo left for the states. He personally thought that Pablo was mentally unbalanced but he did his work. Mateo knew he was going to the States to look at vineyards and that he was picking up one of Santoni's gofers in Florida to go with him.

Galeano told him only a little of what had happened in California, but he did say that Pablo had threatened Santoni. Mateo was surprised that Santoni hadn't shot Pablo himself. He knew how close Galeano and Santoni were. Now Diego wanted revenge. My God, like the middle ages, these boys. Wanting to satisfy his brother's honor. Pablo had no honor. Mateo, personally, was glad he was dead and that it happened in America. He thought Diego had been doing his job, however, he knew he had started to spend more time with Pablo. The other sons were too young to have spent time with Pablo. This last year Diego was dogging his footsteps. He should have seen the signs of hero worship. Why not? He was his big brother and he cut quite a figure with the ladies.

He looked at Galeano, "I have an assistant. Diego doesn't know him. I have had him out in the field watching the men and the books for me. He is very good and looks very innocent. You would never think he was anything but a fresh face. I was going to bring him in and introduce him to you and suggest we move him up. I'm impressed with him. He was also schooled in England and knows one of Santoni's top men.

"He knows my family and is loyal to those he works for, me and you. When we go by the warehouse this afternoon, I will introduce him as one of our new account men. He can also handle himself socially, so he can be in some of the places Diego frequents."

Galeano frowned and looked uncomfortable. Mateo put his hand on his shoulder. "Don't be feeling guilty about, what, spying on your son? Diego is an intense young man, and in his eyes Pablo could do no wrong. We will meet later today."

Mateo arranged by phone to have his young assistant met them at the warehouse. He explained it was to be very low key. He told Miguel what he wanted him to do with Diego. He made it clear that Galeano knew and ordered this. He explained the necessity of this being very secret.

His man Miguel quietly listened and said he understood. He also told him that there was already talk about Diego. How he talked after he had a few drinks at the bars. Yes, he would watch him. Damn, thought Mateo. He too had heard stuff about Diego. He only hoped for his boss's sake it had not gone too far.

When Galeano got back to his home office after the meeting at the warehouse. He sat and thought about the low-keyed meeting with Miguel. Miguel was tall for a Spaniard and blond to boot. He laughed when Galeano remarked on it. He told him he was lucky his father hadn't thrown him back—probably would have if his own grandfather hadn't been a blond. They talked about the business and what Miguel had been doing. Galeano asked him if he would like to come and work more closely with Mateo. They needed to school the younger ones and since he noticed that Miguel was multilingual and had a major in accounting and international finance. He would be very useful.

Pablo and Diego did not go on to school in England. He would be sure his younger sons, and even daughters, did. The older boys professed to love the wine business and wanted to work at that, and of course in the syndicate business later. Now he wondered if his pleasure at having them working with him wasn't selfish and shortsighted. The world was different now. More sophisticated. This trafficking in young women and children hearkened back to the old days of slave trade. Something only the lowest of men did, in countries that were less than civilized.

He reached for his phone. He would call Santoni and wish him a Merry Christmas and ask him his opinion on this. He knew the number he dialed was to Santoni's private office number. A woman with a lovely but businesslike voice answered. "Yes, Mr. Galeano. How can I be of help to you?"

Galeano laughed, "When I finish with my friend Oliver, I will give you my assistant's name and number and you can tell him how to set up this magic system of yours that allows you to see great distances with only a phone."

"I'll be most happy to do that. Let me tell Mr. Santoni you are on the phone."

"Galeano, you old pirate, next thing it will be my secretary you try to steal."

"Is she as pretty as she sounds? If so, beware! I will come for her myself." They chatted a bit then Galeano confessed to Santoni what he had omitted about Pablo's past behavior and his fear for his next oldest, Diego.

"I fear I have been too insular in my little world here in Spain. I won't make that mistake with my other children. I will talk with you later about their further education in England. For now I have curiosity about this thing they call trafficking. I'm sure you know I have taken care of the part of it that Pablo was into. I have also set into motion actions to rid as much of it as possible from Spain. Working with the Federals is not to my liking but one has to do what one can in a situation of this kind."

Santoni smiled to himself and felt greatly relieved that his friend had called and confessed his lack of oversight with his sons. "Yes, I heard you've been busy. I've set into motion similar actions in the other countries where we do business. It is a disgusting situation. We won't get it wiped out over night. I fear where ever there are depraved men we'll have such things."

"But Oliver, does this kind of thing exist so boldly in the United States?"

Oliver laughed, "They may be rich and educated but they have whores and the business of creating whores is worldwide. I do believe if prostitution were legal everywhere, and we put the whores, or shall I say women, in charge, it would be better."

"Yes, Oliver, I agree, I'm not that naïve. It is the stealing of children that must be stopped at all cost. Aren't there organizations of women or something that are devoted to that? I've heard there are. Can you have one of your better educated men get me some information on this. I think this is something the syndicate can help in."

Santoni was quiet for a bit. 'Lord, it is Christmas. What will Elmore and Romano say about this?' "Galeano, let me think on this. Now, are you prepared to spend Christmas with your family? Despite all that has happened, will you be able to make this a good holiday for them?"

"Hum, I hadn't given that the thought it deserves. Thank you for reminding me. I will do that and I will look forward to continuing this conversation later."

After he hung up, Santoni got up and walked to the windows. As he stared down at the Thames as he mused on several thoughts. What were the American legal organizations doing about trafficking? Would Arthur know? Or Jeffery? How high a priority was it for them? How prevalent was it? What did his fellow syndicate leaders in the States think? Hum, his current efforts were directed to Europe and England. The next major meeting of the leadership was later this spring, here in England. He would have his men put a paper together on the problem and its relevance to the syndicate. Have it distributed and ask for feedback.

He fervently believed this nasty business was very bad for the syndicate and its established activities. He smiled to himself, 'Annoy the women of this world and you would deeply pay for it across all countries. Years ago, maybe not so much, but times have changed and information moves around the globe in an instant and women talk.'

Yes, he would talk with Arthur and perhaps, if he agreed, Dr. Paul, and maybe some of the others.

Chapter 8

Saturday morning
Bodega

J oan joined Sister in the kitchen over coffee. "They're all gone, we've an empty house, the silence is deafening," Joan paused. "Can you and I sneak a short ride in before they all come back? I mean are your preparations for dinner this evening done?"

"I was thinking the same thing. I had to laugh when Nancy, Sue, and even Mary just stared at you when you didn't jump at the chance to do a quick shopping run with them."

"Yes," Joan agreed "and then, when Toni walked in and Mary asked her if she wanted to go along, she just glowed with delight."

"It is such a blessing for her to have these lovely women as..." she hesitated.

"Are you looking for the expression, 'role models'?" Joan asked.

"No, it's more than that. It's like loving friends. The age difference doesn't seem to matter. When I watch them all together, all I see are women who like each other and care. They can hug and touch and laugh. Tease each other, and just be warm. We're like that when we're with them. I like it a lot." Sister nodded to herself. "Okay, lets take a quick ride. I'll show you a short cut to Twisted Hills. It's very close, through the woods. Also if everyone is coming to ride this afternoon we don't want to work the horses too much."

It was a comfortable morning, in the high fifties. The forest was alive with small noises and birds in the trees. They were on a forest path that wove through the trees. The saddle leather quietly creaked with the movement of the riders. Joan rode behind on the narrow stretches then joined Sister abreast. They could see the trees thinning out ahead. As they neared the clearing they heard a voice off to their left. "Halt! Who goes there?"

"Don't shoot till you see the whites of their eyes." Another voice said on their right.

"I've got them covered from back here." Yet another voice.

Sister halted. "We surrender. But remember, if you take all our money, there will be no Christmas presents."

They heard a giggle and saw a young boy creep out of the under-brush. "Bet we scared you, huh Sister?" Two more, aged about seven or eight, appeared.

"I sure didn't hear you coming. You're getting much better at this hunting stuff." She turned to Joan, "You remember the Foster's son, Jacob. These must be your cousins, here to visit over the holidays."

"Yeah, we're helping Mr. Arthur and Jeffery with the security system. They're trying to find us with some new heat-seeking stuff. He's in contact with us," He held up a small phone. "They found you instead, and told us to sneak up on you if we could. We did, too."

"Must be because the horses present such a large heat picture. Jacob, you go tell Jeffery that's why he found us."

"Yeah, that'll really impress them." They dashed off and disap-peared into the trees. Sister rode out a bit further and they could see the rows of grapes stretched out before them.

Sister pointed off to the right, "That way will take you to the house at Twisted Hills."

"Come, I'll show you a small stream that runs between the vine-yards. It then winds down past my place."

"Those were really well-mannered children. They show respect without fear. You taught them that, didn't you?"

"No, Joan, we all taught them manners. Can't have loving chil-dren, allow them to run free and grow, if they don't have manners and know obedience. We all set the same limits, and if differences arise, the adults discus the situation and come up with one solution. The parents are the final judge. My God, between the two families there are," she paused and counted, "Thirteen kids; plus all the cous-ins who come, the vineyard help's kids who come to visit and the children who are here at harvest time."

"That's a lot. I noticed them around the pool last summer. But not that many."

"They took turns. Their mothers organized the traffic." Sis-ter turned. "Even Mary would faint if they all came at once." She laughed. "Last summer, right after Mary arrived we were having

Sunday coffee on the deck at seven a.m. The question came up of the use of the pool. After some prodding, I finally told her how Babs used the pool—the children and all. She asked if I hid the children when she arrived. She insisted we go back to the same schedule we used every other year.

"I fell in love." Sister laughed. "We all did. It became home again for all of us since Babs's death. You were here last summer, you saw how it was. Sue added to it by playing with the children. It was a blessing to them and they to her. When Ghost, Babs's cat, found Sue at the piano, that was like a rebirth around here. One for all of us. Look, there's my place up that slope from the creek. Would you like to see it?"

"Very much. Mary said it was a jewel."

"Hum, we tried, Babs and I, to make it homey. Toni stayed with me when she wasn't at the Fosters' or the Salinases'. Kids do a lot of sleepovers. Even here at this little place. The only rule was advance notice. No surprises for any of us. We all wanted to know where everyone was."

The house was a soft cream trimmed in a soft green. It blended into the trees and flowers around it. A large porch wrapped two sides. You could enter through the front or the back side of the porch. The house sort of hunkered down among the trees. It was private and cozy and warm.

The floor plan was open. The main entrance was into the living room, with a large centered fireplace facing you, with the room flowing right into a dining area that became part of the kitchen as it turned to the back right side. On the left as you came in were pocket doors standing open to a small library that opened into a master bedroom a connecting bath and smaller bedroom. A hall flowed alongside these room and took you into the kitchen. The porch off the side of the kitchen opened on to a barbecue area and outdoor sitting and eating space.

"How clever! The fireplace divides the house front and back and the other rooms side to side. Cozy yet private and open. Who designed it?"

"Both Babs and I. When Mary saw it, she said it was identical to the home of a friend from her child hood but on a smaller scale. I was afraid she would immediately move in."

"I don't blame her. Yet you stay at the main house a lot. Is that only to keep Mac company?"

"No, Joan, I truly love that house. It was my first real home. Living at the top of the house, in the attic room, with those two huge windows at either end was heaven. I know Nancy loves it when she's here. It gives her peace while she paints. It gave me a secret hideaway of my own, with only one entrance into the room but two ways down the two sets of stairs, front and back, if I wanted to escape. When Nancy leaves, I air out the faint paint odor and move back in.

"Joan, I felt so safe, yet free. Babs made it clear to the children that was my private space they were not to enter unless invited. The house is so large, they had enough room of their own they didn't bother me. After a year or two, she had me going to school and I acquired more books and needed more space, privacy and quiet. We talked and drew and drew. Then she had a young architect come and spend time with me and we rode in the woods and found the spot and I told him what I really wanted and between us we created it. Now, mind you, Babs was over our shoulders most of the time. When I walked through it in my mind it finally felt just right."

She spun in a circle, "See? Here it is, just like I saw it."

Joan watched her and could see the beautiful young woman as she was then. Not that much changed. More filled out but still slim and strong and obviously very competent. Very much her own person. "Are you ever lonely?"

"I missed Babs, as I told you. Yet it's hard to be too lonely when you are running a vineyard... rather, two vineyards. Now, it is all changed again." Sister almost twirled about the room. "Now I get to go to Europe and Portugal and learn how to make Port and Champagne. I also have a whole new large, wonderful family." She stopped and looked at Joan, "Also a new, and what is turning out to be a close, confidant."

Joan smiled, "Yes, I would love to be your confidant. Such a lovely word. Carries so much meaning." She nodded to herself.

"Good, I'm glad. I think we should start back. I've enjoyed sharing my home with you. I'll fix us lunch or something here. Maybe an all-girls' day after Christmas."

After a quick fix-your-own lunch, with much chatter and rushing to get into riding clothes, Sister chased the ladies out to get the horses ready, telling them she would join them after she had evening dinner preparations in hand. She told them she didn't need help. There were people coming to help prepare and serve later.

She heard the dogs barking and looked out the window to see Romano and Elmore arrive.

'Oh, what handsome young men. Well, not that young they are in their late thirties, Elmore maybe in his forties.' She eyed them and smiled to herself, well-fitting riding britches really did show men and women at their best. She remembered making this remark to Arthur last summer then almost giggling at herself. He told her not to be embarrassed. He was in full agreement and enjoyed the scenery as well.

He, Mac, Jeffery and the other men rode in denim. They could all ride well but not dressage. She had watched both Arthur and Jeffery eye the women when they rode, and the men as well. Smiling to herself she said, 'Sister, I bet it won't take much to get them started. One day when they are both here without Mary and the girls.'

Elmore walked up to the house carrying a box. He entered through the kitchen. "Sister, good day to you. Will you put this in the library for me? It contains some things that Santoni wanted Mac, Arthur, Jeffery, Mary, Romano, you, and me to have. Perhaps when you see them arrive you will call me and we can come in, and in private, get on with it."

Sister took the box, nodding, "I'll do it."

About an hour later Mac, Arthur, and Jeffery drove up. They went to the arena and stood at the fence with the others who weren't riding. Sister was leaning on the fence and whistled, and waved Romano, Elmore and Mary to her. They dismounted and Sister told them and the new arrivals they were all wanted in the house. She told Sue, Joan and Toni they could continue to ride and the rest would be right back.

After they all settled in the library. Elmore stood and opened the box and announced that this was a present to all of them from Santoni. He, with Romano's help gave each of them a small box with a gold tie around it. The boxes were white for the women and black for the men. After they had opened their boxes he told them exactly what Santoni told him after they had gotten theirs.

He and Romano both watched Jeffery. He carefully took the gun apart, examined the works and the bullets, whistled. "Wow, I've never seen one like this!" He looked at Elmore and then Romano. "I don't suppose I ever will." He said with raised eyebrows.

Romano smiled. "It is not on the market. We hope it never will be, except in a very controlled way."

"Sister, look, mine is black on one side and white on the other."

"For formal evening wear, I bet," said Sister. They both laughed.

Mac and Arthur watched them and looked at each other. "Lord save us," said Mac. "Wouldn't you know that would be the first thing they would say."

"It could never be detected by airport screening, or any other more sophisticated machines," Romano stated.

Jeffery eyed Romano, "There are rumors about a private English company that does research on material like this for the Crown. The founders name is Vargas. Any relation?"

"They don't work for the Crown. Private research only. This is a model." He smiled at Jeffery. "Don't worry! It has been tested. It is very safe. Safer then what you are currently using. Oliver wants everyone to become familiar with it. However, you all are not to practice too much with it, as the bullets are very expensive. Use your own guns for practice. Further, Jeffery, it does not have the stopping power the one you carry does. It's for an emergency only."

He went on and explained why Oliver sent them and that he wanted the three of them to have them when they went to Europe. He wanted Mary to be armed as well. He explained the scuttlebutt out of Spain about Pablo's younger brother. He further felt responsible for bringing this mess onto them. They all chatted a bit longer and left to put their gifts away. Except Jeffery and Romano who stayed and eagerly talked more guns and materials.

Mary and Sister looked back at them from the door. Sister raised an eyebrow, "Brothers perhaps?" She whispered.

"Amazing. Just what Jeffery needed." Mary replied.

Chapter 9

Christmas at Bodega

Saturday evening's dinner was another of Sister's culinary masterpieces: a standing rack of lamb, asparagus tips, new potatoes, all the sauces, salads, rolls, and a variety of deserts. Mac picked the red and white wines. They all ate and talked about the day.

Sister and Mac told them, over port, they would like to do Christmas Eve and Day like it used to be done, if no one objected. Mary asked them to describe that for them and quickly added that she had no objections.

Sister looked at Mac and he nodded for her to go ahead. "Christmas Eve is Monday and the families, the Fosters and Salinases and children, all go to early church services. They go to the children's mass at three p.m. Then they all come here bearing and receiving gifts and have a buffet dinner. No one is allowed to open their gifts till the next morning. Then we all gather in the main living room and sing carols, and eat wonderful deserts." She looked around. "Any questions so far?"

"Does this include the cousins as well?" Joan asked.

"No, they go to their own homes and come back later the next day to spend time and show off what they got, with their cousins, aunts and uncles."

Mac took over. "The next morning, at dawn, we all gather in the living room and open gifts."

"At dawn?" asked Nancy.

He stared at her. "Yes, young woman. At dawn!" Nancy shut her mouth and just nodded.

Sister said. "Mac, Arthur, and Mary wanted you, Elmore, and Romano to be here for both Christmas Eve and Day. So, we will put Sue and Joan together—they can share Sue's room for the night. Assuming, of course, that you Elmore and Romano will join us. Christmas dinner is at two p.m." She looked at them both. They just stared at her and nodded.

"That's it then. See how easy that was. Any questions?"

Mary snickered. "They wouldn't dare."

"Is that a question, Ms. Mary?" asked Mac.

"No, sir."

"Good. That winds up dinner and our announcement."

"Excuse me, sir." Elmore said.

"Yes, Elmore."

"Romano and I checked, and were told there are no plans for to-morrow, Sunday afternoon. We've made tentative plans for you all to join us for an early dinner at Santoni's place. Will that be okay? We checked it out with Sister and Mary. Will it be okay with the rest of you?"

They all chimed in with agreement, with most asking what they could bring. Was it formal? How could they help? Sister smiled at Mary, who stood up and said, "Good, it's all settled. Yes, it is dress up, but not long dresses. Now, Sue, will you play for us?" She paused, looking down at Ghost sitting at Sue's feet, then added, "Sister, can we help clean up?"

"No, it is all done. I'll just make a quick check and join you all."

Ghost, walking in front of Sue, sprang up on top of the baby grand piano and stretched out. Romano sat in a chair next to Mary. He looked at Mary, smiled as he asked, "Does the cat play too? Or sing, perhaps?"

Mary grinned and told him that Ghost belonged to Mac's wife. After Babs died, Ghost made herself scarce except to be fed by Sister. When Sue got here, she began playing the piano one afternoon when no one was home. She hadn't played since the death of her sister last spring. Sue said while she was playing, she looked up and there was Ghost lying on the piano, looking down at her. Sister told us Babs was a concert pianist, and Ghost occupied the piano when Babs played.

"Since last summer, Ghost has returned to the house full time. She generally follows either Sister or Mac. She will go to Nancy's room at the top of the house, with my dogs and watch her paint. She has also taken to sitting on the arena fence when we ride and practice dressage. Another of Bab's loves."

Sue began with a few light show tunes and when Joan sat down she started with carols. A few moments later, Sister joined them with her beautiful soprano complementing Joan's alto. After a bit Mary leaned toward Romano. "Do you sing?"

"I can."

"Please, I would like that."

Romano walked quietly up beside Sister, and added a wonderful tenor, and minutes later Jeffery joined with his bass. Arthur sat down by Mary and held her hand. Soon Elmore, Nancy and Toni joined the singers. Mac sat across the room and just smiled, with the dogs at his feet.

Mary whispered to Arthur, "I think that gun cracked Jeffery's shell."

"You mean, it opened him to a full family."

"Yes, look at them. Have you ever seen such warm, beautiful men and women? I'm sorry Santoni is missing this."

Arthur thought a moment. "Yes, I bet he is too."

Sunday late afternoon.

Santoni's house was beautiful. It stood back from the cliff, overlooking the ocean. Mac told them it was built back when old oak and timber were easy to come by. The windows were wide and sunk back into the casement like they were hiding. The inside was comfortably furnished, and the fireplace deeply set into the stone wall.

They were greeted with the tiny white lights along the entrance and partially hidden in the trees. This theme was carried throughout the interior of the house. Mary smiled when she saw it and edged up to Sister. "Busy, weren't you?"

"What matters is, do you like it?"

"Yes. Do the boys?" Sister nodded.

Sister and Joan were dressed in shimmering white for Joan and red for Sister. The others were in pleasing combinations of complementary colors, the men in dark suits. Champagne was served in tall crystal glasses that sparkled and glowed in the firelight.

Dinner was pork tenderloin and a wonderful key lime pie to end

it. Then Elmore put some lovely dance music on and everyone ro-
tated around the floor. Toni put a tango on and Elmore put his arms
out to Sister. They made the room sparkle, and soon they were joined
by Romano and Toni. They switched, and Sue danced with Romano
and Joan with Elmore. Jeffery looked at Nancy and raised his eyebrows and she nodded and they made the others look like beginners.

Mary, Mac, and Arthur watched and admired the young ones.
When a waltz started Arthur spun Mary around the floor and everyone applauded until Joan and Mac took the floor. Each couple
tried to outdo the other in elegance. Finally they all stretched out in
front of the fireplace and sighed, all in agreement that they must do
this again soon. They laughed on the way home and even sang some
lively Christmas songs.

Christmas Eve Monday was busy. The dining room was prepared to handle a large buffet. Mary watched in amazement as Sister directed traffic with ease. When she asked what she could do. Sister gave her a hug and said it was all choreographed, from years of
practice. Toni came in just then and told Sister she was going to the
children's mass. Mary asked her if she could go with her. Toni was
joyous. She paused. "Can I drive the Mercedes?"

Mary said, "Yes." Sister rolled her eyes as she watched them
waltz out the door together.

Arthur came up behind her. "You know Sister, this may be the
first time in years that Mary has gone to Mass."

Sister looked at him. "Hum, I can understand that. It being a children's mass makes it easier. Did you get all the presents for the children into the library?"

"I did. Now what?"

"They will all be back here in less than 2 hours, the mass is shorter for the kids..." She was said as they walked out of the room.

It wasn't long before Elmore and Romano arrived carrying garment bags. Nancy appeared and showed them their room.They also
had bags of presents for the adults that went under the trees plus
bags for the kids and their parents that went into the library. Jeffery
helped them with the bags and they settled down in the library to
talk horses and riding. Jeffery peppered Elmore and Romano with

questions about dressage and did not see Sister leaning on the door frame listening with a smile on her face until, Arthur came and put his arm around her waist, and smiled down at her.

"You'll tell Mary?" Sister said.

"Can't wait." They joined the men and Arthur said, "We're all set, won't be long before we are descended upon."

Jeffery's eyes were shining. "I must be honest, I've had a number of lovely holidays with Mary and Arthur, but nothing like this. I can't wait till the kids get here." He paused, "Sister, I must confess, I went over the allowance you suggested I spend, but I love these kids. Sister did you tell anyone how I had them stalk you in the woods?"

"No. I thought I'd wait till you mentioned it. I knew you would. You're like Arthur, two grown men still playing cops and robbers."

"Me? Never. It was his idea." Arthur pointed at Jeffery.

Romano looked at Jeffery. "What did you do?" Off they went on a discussion of Jeffery's new security toy. Soon they heard the dogs barking, followed by cries of joy and running feet.

Joan, Sue and Nancy welcomed everyone at the door and the party began.

First everyone exchanged gifts with much begging to open just one. Firm NOs, from the parents and Sister, ended that. The children had pooled their money and bought one gift for each of the adults with the family names attached on the 'from' line. These were put in the living room with the other adult gifts. Jeffery made a big thing about squeezing his and trying to guess what it was. Then they gathered by the tree in the library. There were 13 large bags with gifts and the each had a child's name attached. Mary and Sister handed them out. They took some gifts out and looked and guessed. One of the youngest sat at Elmore's feet and whispered to him, when she handed him a gift from her bag. He picked her up. Set her on his lap, gave her a kiss on the cheek ruffled her hair and said, "No," with a big smile.

"That one will be the death of me when she gets older," said Luciana.

"She is now," laughed Betty Foster. "Look who she learned it from."

Luciana did a big denial in a burst of Spanish, which Elmore answered in Spanish. He finished by saying, "I would take this lovely any day," as he bounced the child on his lap.

They all moved to the buffet, loaded plates and found seats on the floor or chairs. Everyone was talking and eating. The children each tried to con a different adult into telling them what they bought them. Finally, Toni said, "We must move to the living room, and Sue will accompany the children while they sing for you. They have been practicing."

The children gathered around and in front of the piano. Some standing some sitting. Toni stood off to the side but in front, and directed the chorus. Ghost was stretched out on the piano and the Shepherds on the floor near Mary. They sang from serious songs like "Come all ye Faithful" to "Jingle Bells." Everyone applauded and some even joined in.

Then Toni asked Sister if she and Joan would start "Silent Night." Elmore, Jeffery, Romano, Nancy, and the parents joined them on the second verse, then the children finished it off. Mary, Mac and Arthur stayed in their seats and quietly enjoyed it all. They realized nothing was expected of them, rather, it was a gift to them. A wonderful Christmas gift.

Chapter 10

Christmas morning

It was five a.m. Mary was in the kitchen pouring a cup of coffee when Sister came in the back door. "Getting a jump on things, are we?" quipped Sister.

Mary set a second cup down and poured for Sister. "Wouldn't take that pleasure from you. I woke and was so excited I just had to get up. Felt like a kid." She smiled.

"I have to say I did too." She paused. "I wanted to open just one, like the kids."

They both laughed. "When will the families start opening gifts?"

"There's a light on in the Salinases' kitchen. I saw it as I drove up. Luciana won't let them start till everyone is up." She looked up as Nancy entered carrying to two large packages.

She leaned them against the center cooking table and poured a cup of coffee. She then looked at the two of them and finally handed each a package. "Will you open these for me now, please? With just the three of us here."

Mary and Sister looked at each other and nodded. Sister got hers open first. It was a magnificent picture of Sister astride Simon. Her head was up, alert, staring right at the observer. The horse was facing away at a small angle.

Sister and Mary just looked at it in silence. Finally Mary said, "You are truly beautiful, Sister. I don't know who is the more majestic, you or Simon."

Sister stood very still looking and they saw tears in her eyes. She turned and hugged Nancy and gave her a kiss on the cheek.

Mary picked her package up. It too was a painting. Mary was sitting and staring off to her left. She was very tan, her hair was sun-streaked and longer than she was wearing it now. Her eyes were a vivid blue with a touch of green, her shirt white with blue shading. She wasn't sad, but one might call the expression pensive. "Hum, I was younger then. I know that expression. The feeling is known to me. I didn't know how observant you were, my love. I will always treasure this. I can remember those years. I was quite handsome, wasn't I?" She wrapped Nancy in a hug and a kiss.

Nancy looked at the two of them. "I certainly didn't mean to turn you two so, so serious. Smile, damn it."

Finally, Sister moved and poured more coffee for everyone. "I didn't know you saw us as such beauties. Nancy, I can't speak for Mary but it is such an honor to be seen like that in a portrait. Like Mary, I can remember me in that pose. It is how, I'm sure, I looked right before the start of a dressage show. Oh yes. Poised, contained, completely in charge. Simon looked like that as well. You are a beautiful talented woman. Thank you. How did you do that? I mean, to catch me so perfectly."

"I watched you a lot, and I have a camera I dearly love. Mary, I have known for years and sketched her many times without her knowledge. I loved this particular look of hers. Although now, she appears more content and happier. That is unless you catch her when she is ready to kill you."

"What's going on here? Who broke the rule about opening presents early? Oh my! Look at that." Arthur said as he entered the kitchen. "How wonderful. How perfect! Nancy, you said…"

"Hush Arthur, this is Mary's Christmas present, so she won't forget how she looked when she was at the University. Do you like it?"

"How could I not? I love the woman at any age and always will." He hugged Mary, then examined Sister's portrait. "Sister, yes, that is my Sister. Perfectly done, Nancy. Let me move them to the living room, to the piano, so Sister and Mary can reign over the present opening."

Sister said, "I have fruit, buns and rolls. Let me set them up in the dining room. Everyone will be down soon and Toni will be here in a minute."

"I can help," Nancy and Mary said in unison.

It wasn't long before everyone was up, grabbing coffee and heading for the living room. They all stopped and gazed at the paintings on the piano. Joan couldn't help but walk up and touch them. She let her fingers linger on Sister's face then on Mary's. Sue walked up to her, "Is the analyst inside you very busy? Do you just see or absorb? Perhaps there isn't a difference."

Joan put her arm around her and said, "I would love to own both those paintings."

"I can understand that. Now to the presents."

Everyone was delighted. The women had to try all the perfumes, there was no talk of swapping. Sister said, "You English gentleman are very good in matching the scent to the lady. How did you do it?"

Elmore and Romano grinned. "We shopped together at a very special store. We described each of you and requested two suggestions. We took both, one from each of us. Although, Toni, I was afraid we might get arrested when we got to you. Elmore quickly explained you were our baby sister."

"Hum Toni, let me smell again. I want to remember what being your age smelled like," Joan said as she held out her hand.

Arthur smiled. He looked the box over carefully and asked, "Isn't this where the Queen shops?"

Jeffery in a gruff voice said, "Ha! I knew you didn't do it alone." Everyone laughed. "But what I want to know is who picked out these beautiful boots?" He looked at Arthur's, "They're every bit a nice as Arthur's." There was silence.

Toni, grinning, said, "Don't ask, don't tell."

Arthur had left the room and on returning was carrying a beautiful black saddle. He walked over to Sister and set it down. Sister looked at the saddle and touched it and then caressed it. She felt the leather and rubbed it with her finger and thumb like you would a piece of silk. She looked at the name etched in small fine letters on the silver. "It's a Passier Sirius. I've always wanted one. It is like owning a Bentley." She got to her feet and kissed Arthur and then Mary. Turning to the rest of the room she announced, "For me, it is better."

Jeffery stood up and handed her a box. "This is the trimmings— or do you call them the accessories?—to Mary's and Arthur's gift." Inside was beautiful black tack, a blanket and riding crop in sterling, with her name engraved on the handle.

Sister kissed Jeffery and then spun around and said like a very young woman, "I don't know what to do. I don't have anything to wear with this, this…" she waved at the saddle and accessories.

Joan stood and hugged her, "Mustn't worry, my dear, we'll just go shopping." Everyone laughed and got on with the rest of the gifts. Of course the women all tried on Mary's diamond and emerald dinner ring and earrings. She was speechless, and that only got worse when she opened the pearl earrings and necklace from Mac. Mary burst out and said, "I could make a good down payment on another vineyard with these!"

Finally, the boys asked when could they go and thank the kids for their gifts and see how they liked theirs. Sister had put the turkey in the oven and dinner would be after three p.m. She told them they would all go now. First to the Salinases, then the Fosters. She would call them and tell them when to expect company.

After everyone finished the cheers and thanks, Mary and Sister snuck out and went back, to work on dinner. When Mary had asked her earlier who was helping with dinner. Sister told her they wouldn't have the help today. She said families should have Christmas together. No problem, Mary had replied. She had done dinner for more people than this.

It wasn't long before Joan, Nancy, Toni, and Sue arrived. Sister delegated tasks and the timing: cleaning up the living room, setting the table, fixing the side dishes. They all worked and laughed and nibbled as they went. They teased Sister about the need to go all black with Simon.

She said no, she would let Mary do that using her saddle. The conversation went on about color coordination at Dressage shows.

At five p.m. everyone had pushed their chairs back a bit and drank some of the port Elmore and Romano brought the men for Christmas. Elmore felt his phone vibrate. He looked at the face and it was Santoni. He told them who was calling and stood to leave the table when Mary asked him to put Santoni on speaker. He explained to Santoni and Mary spoke over him saying, "Merry Christmas Oliver, I wish you were here."

"Yes, my dear. I must say, so do I. Is Arthur sharing the port with you?"

"Sharing, ha!" Said Arthur. "That is not the word I would use. The fine Christmas present from the boys is rapidly disappearing. Thank you for the guns. They are beautiful. Jeffery can hardly leave his alone."

"Do you like your present from Arthur, Mary?"

"It is breathlessly beautiful. Did you help pick it out?"

"No, that man has exquisite taste. He has you, doesn't he? Sister, do you like the saddle?"

"What's not to like? Did you pick it out?"

"No, Mac did. He called me to be sure that was the very best. Arthur and Mary wouldn't have anything but the best for you. I also want to wish a Merry Christmas to the other beautiful women at the table."

A chorus of voices could be heard. "Tomorrow is a working day for me, I know it's not for you, but I need some information. Jeffery, I can establish a secure line here, can you do the same somewhere there, where I can talk with you, Arthur, Romano, and Elmore?"

"Yes, of course. Do you have a time in mind?"

They discussed timing and then Mary asked. "May I sit in, please? I'm considered trustworthy, and these two do belong to me."

There was a moment of silence. Then they could hear Santoni laugh, "Yes, indeed they do. Now as I reflect on it, Mac and Sister should sit in as well. Now let me have Elmore for a private moment. I look forward to sharing a meal with you all some time in the New Year."

Mary sat at the table musing on the conversation with Santoni as all the others helped clear dishes away. She stood and called, "Elmore, come with me into the library."

She shut the door behind him. "Now, in as few words as possible, tell me what it is Santoni wants to talk to us about." She watched him withdraw. "Now don't do that and do not fidget. Just in simple words tell me the basic content of tomorrow's phone call."

Elmore was Santoni's top man and Mary knew it. She watched him weigh and balance.

"He wants to ask Jeffery, Mac, and Arthur what they know about trafficking here in the United States." He stopped.

Mary said, "And?" and waved her hand in a circular motion in the air.

Elmore looked down. Finally he said, "Pablo's youngest brother, Diego, is making noise about seeking vengeance for Pablo. Separate from that, his father wants Santoni to help him get rid of any trafficking on the continent." He paused and watched Mary.

"So, how do we fit in?"

"He wants to ask Jeffery and Arthur about what kind of problem this is here in the US. What do people think, if they think about it at all? He wants all of you to be alert to the fact that Diego may, by some stretch of the imagination, be a danger to you and others. He has a small concern about Arthur, Mac, and Sister traveling in France and Portugal. Mind you, very small, as they will be nowhere near Spain and one of us will be with them."

Mary thought about what he had told her. She got up and walked to the window. He sat and watched her carefully. She was a very bright woman, and clever, as Santoni had told him. He could see her processing and even planning. What a general she would make!

She turned and sat. "Elmore I want you to call Santoni back. Tell him I want Sue, Nancy, and Joan at the meeting." Elmore started to speak, but she waved him down. "Joan is a brilliant, and a famous telepath, well connected in the female world. Sue is just as good with telepathy, and is a clairvoyant who works with the police in New York State. Nancy is sensitive beyond description and very close to Jeffery, and even closer to me. Together we are a powerful group of women.

"Your search for information about trafficking concerns women and children. Not men, unless we are into male slavery. Therefore you need the best information, theoretically, you can get. In addition, their lives were on the line that night as well. So I want you to call Santoni, tell him I said it will be all or none."

Elmore sat and looked at Mary. She could see him processing her statements. He nodded and said. "I'll do that now. May I do it in here?"

Mary nodded, stood and walked out, shutting door behind her.

Chapter 11

Everyone was gathered in the library. Jeffery was handling the phone. When it rang he picked up and said, "London?"

"Yes."

"Hold for a minute, please." He paused, fiddled with some equipment, and then said, "Good day, Sir. This line is secure now."

"Good, I hope this time is satisfactory with everyone, I wouldn't want to interfere with a wine tasting, Sister."

"Not till ten. We have time. We also have able assistants."

"What I want to know, rather let me say, need to know, is something about the problem of trafficking in humans in the States. As background, let me tell you what has been happening here since last fall." He explained he had sent out word to the people he was associated with, to carefully check that they did not have any involvement at all in this business. If they did, it was to cease immediately. He was soon told it was being eradicated in Spain forcefully. Further, he was being asked if he would assist in helping to stop this activity everywhere.

"My major interest is the children. By children, I mean those who are considered underaged—I believe that is 18 years. I'm not talking about prostitution unless it's enforced slavery. There are people who think if one engages is some activities that the law considers illegal, that they will do anything. I assure you that is not so. Further I consider trafficking in children, or forcibly any human, to be totally objectionable.

"Some of my colleagues asked me to find out if this is a problem in the States. So that is my first question, mainly directed to Jeffery."

"It didn't used to be at least noticeable, some years ago, but it has rapidly increased. They, the captives, have come across our border with Mexico. Also from South America or Africa and elsewhere in ship, in their holds or in sealed containers. Some ships anchor off shore and send them ashore in boats. Some have been known to keep them in abandoned oil drilling platforms. Those nearer the coast of Florida are the most prized. They can then be loaded onto RIB'S, small rigid inflatable boats, then the people can be offloaded on the beaches at night. Florida has miles of beaches in uninhabited areas. The women, children and even men are then taken to warehouses and later moved to the next site by trucks.

"Many of these men are from the country of origin or speak the language. They stay with what they call the product, till delivery, or until someone else can communicate. The top people are generally Americans not necessary white. It is a very lucrative business, as was the African slave trade."

"What happens to the kids when the traffickers are caught?"

Jeffery said, "That can be very sad. If they were kidnapped they can be returned to their family. However many are sold by their family or tribes. We try to find agencies is their county who will help in these cases. NPOs—non-profit organizations—are getting more involved in helping these people. It is a very sad affair. It is only in the past few years that it has gained much public attention."

"Tell me about the public attention. That is my second question." Santoni said.

"There are groups who want the government to pass a trafficking law that will put these people out of business. I'm not sure what the laws being considered contain."

"Mr. Santoni, this is Joan. That is not all that is being done. Maybe all on the official or legal level. However, the women in this country are banding together to get the word out to other women. They are saying to them, don't hire foreign women who are not credentialed. Go to the authorities and find out if the agency is licensed. They are told to go quietly. To contact the police if they find they are not. Further if the police don't respond, they're to go to one of the women's groups who will investigate further. We believe some of the police are paid not to respond. When this happens they go to the press and make as much noise as possible.

"It's shameful in this country to be associated with child abuse, as well as illegal. To stop it takes public exposure at the highest level possible. One may be caught with drugs or even stealing but to be accused of pedophilia will ruin you forever. Sexual assault to a minor, anyone under eighteen years, is enough to label you as a predator and earn a long jail term."

"Joan," Santoni asked, "is this just among women of the professional set or is it more general in the population?"

Sue chimed in. "This is Sue. I think it started out at the professional level, but in New York it has rapidly moved into the mainstream. Also among the police, in the suburbs, there's a growing awareness of something not being quite right. In the northern areas of New York City, in the wealthy areas, where more servants are hired, the hiring price is getting higher and higher. These women speak poor English. When they leave work someone picks them up and brings them back the next day. When they are asked about this, they say it's a bus service that the employment agency hires. So no one knows where they live. It has to be some distance away since one can't afford the local rental prices."

"How do you know this, Sue?" asked Santoni.

"The police had a woman they found on the side of the road. She had been beaten, and apparently ran away. When she wouldn't tell them anything they called me. I spent some time with her and kept getting mental pictures of other women who were very frightened and had said to her not to tell. I finally told her it was okay, tell me why those women didn't want her to talk to me. She asked me if the sprits spoke to me about the other women. I told her the spirits wanted her to be safe and to save the others.

"The upshot was these men were keeping her and ten others in and old farm house, feeding them next to nothing, telling them to eat at work. They told them if they didn't obey, they would never see their children again. The police found the farm house, and then followed the men to where they were living, and raided both the house the men lived in and the farm house.

"The authorities got hold of the police in the country where these women had been kidnapped from. In this case one of the women was related to one of the top police officials so there was no retaliation. At least yet."

"Mr. Santoni, it is a very complicated situation." Jeffery said, "Sometimes it is the countries officials themselves who are involved in the slave ring. Also, as Joan told you, the women who are working against this believe that public exposure both here and in the country of origin is the only way to stop this, especially if the local official are exposed."

Santoni was quiet for a while. Everyone waited. "Your society is very socially conscious, I mean they care a lot about what others think. Have these women gone to the media and had programs put on about this?"

"This is Nancy. I have friends in New York City who work in the media. There's a push to do what you are talking about. It's a slow process. The best source for serious work, is what we call PBS, Public Broadcasting System. It is supported with grants that pay for these programs If you can get the public interested then the commercial market can get shows developed that have that as a theme."

"So, it is a question of money over morals?"

"Is it not always, Oliver?"

"Ah, my friend Mary. You get right to the heart of the issue. It has many facets. May I make a request? I know you all are on vacation, but that doesn't interfere with your thought processes. Like chatting over coffee, like plotting the demise of this pestilence. Since it is much more then something the police authorities can deal with, it obviously will take a much broader approach. May I suggest, when you have time, you give some thought to this. Stretch yourselves beyond worrying about the cost of any idea, lets call it a campaign. What will it take in total, and how many areas will need to be attacked at once?

"Arthur, you're the finance man, maybe you could offer some suggestions. No?"

"Do you play chess, Oliver?"

"Yes, and I love to have more than one game going at once. I bet Sister does as well. "

"I settle on one at a time, Oliver."

"Good, but the concept is similar. One major goal, many men on the board and many ways to get to the goal while warding off others. I can only say I'm sorry I'm not there to play with you. I'll observe. I also tell you it is not a game. I think that is all for now. I'll look forward to talking with you all. Unless you have questions. No? Then, till later."

Mary looked at Arthur. His eyes were alert and shining. You

could see ideas spinning and turning. She turned and saw Sister watching him as well. Sister looked at Mary, raised her eyebrows, smiled, gave a bit of a nod. "I think work calls. Wine-tasting work."

Mary followed Sister and said, "Can I ride with you?"

Joan walked up behind them: "Me too!" and was joined by Nancy and Sue.

Mary soon said, "If we could tape the thoughts in this car right now, I bet we would have compete plans ready to go." They all laughed.

"I can hardly contain myself," said Sue.

"Me either," Nancy echoed her.

"For clarity, may I humbly suggest we all just put it in writing? You can use a tape recorder if it helps. I hate to be priggish about this," Joan said, "Having just finished a book, I can assure you these wonderful ideas need to be put in writing, right now or very soon, and individually. Then, and only then, can we compare and build."

Mary turned, looking at Joan. "You're right. Think while we work, then record or make notes on the sales slips." They all changed the subject and when they arrived at Twisted Hills they promptly were flooded with work.

Sister walked with Mary, "It's the holiday season. Presents for the forgotten, and New Year's coming very fast, the holiday crowd leaving for home soon. We will be busy the next few days."

Arthur said, "Elmore, Romano will you stay a moment longer. Jeffery, Mac, I'll be along in a few minutes."

He shut the door behind the other men. "You can get Oliver back on the phone or choose to answer a few questions on your own."

Elmore eyed Arthur, "Such as?"

"What precipitated this call? Do you know?"

Elmore thought a moment. "I think he would have told you himself, but there were too many people present. The Don, Galeano, Pablo's father is a very old friend of Oliver's. He called him and told him what he had found out about his son Pablo in the past months. We knew the Don had initiated a cleanup in Spain of all trafficking.

"He recently became very concerned about his next oldest son, Diego, who has been talking about revenge for the death of his brother, Pablo. The boy spent time with Pablo learning the business, and got into drugs and booze as well. The Don asked Oliver to help him and others get the trafficking stopped in Europe. Then he asked him how bad it was in the States, and would he find out for him. He wants Oliver to help him get all the members of their association to work together to stop this business." He stopped talking and watched Arthur.

"Hum." Arthur paused and thought a minute. "I don't mean to be rude. I do believe Oliver finds this business to be more than distasteful. It could also reflect very badly on others in his business if they were to be associated with it in any way."

"True, however, the Don is really pushing this. He is very angry and deeply offended that a member of his family could be involved is something this nasty. He is an old-world man with high standards. Women and children are held apart from any business and to be cherished. You see it is much more than business."

Arthur nodded. "Thank you," he smiled. "I think you two will be Oliver's research associates and collaborators with the ladies." He watched Elmore frown. Arthur put his hand on Elmore's shoulder, "You mustn't be concerned. I think you will find it to be a very educational exercise. I would liken it to being fellows, assigned to the top female professors in the college."

Chapter 12

Jeffery and Arthur had arranged with the Sheriff of Sonoma to use their indoor shooting range. The Sheriff told them Friday at noon would be a good time. People were either at lunch or on the road. There were five shooting positions. Jeffery told Romano and Elmore they would use four and leave the last one for practice with the new guns. He wanted to collect the bullets from the new guns, as they were made from the same material as the gun—not something they wanted to leave lying about.

Sister and Mary shared a position. Joan had come along with them. Mary asked if Joan could shoot. If so, did she want to? Joan smiled and said she would love to, and yes, she did shoot. She told them she was raised around horses and guns. Mary had an automatic, a Beretta. Sister had the same gun. Joan eyed them both, "Is it ESP, or do we all just have the same good taste?"

"I have revolver, a five-shot Taurus and a Deringer at home, plus of course shotguns and rifles. Arthur got me this last summer—said it was lighter and easier to carry, and he wanted me to carry it when I was out riding. I practiced some last fall when I got home. I'm not ready for a tournament, but I can hit the silhouette most of the time from 25 feet." She then proceeded to do just that. One head shot, the rest to the upper body. "That's enough practice. Your turn, Sister." She pull the paper target to herself and put a new one up, then reloaded her gun for Joan.

Sister put her gun down, flexed her fingers, picked it up and put five in the head. She was done before anyone could watch properly. "Must be the gun, Mary. Arthur got me this last year. Like you, he said he would feel better if I had a proper firearm. I had a revolver, but he didn't like it. Then after the trouble with Toni's father, Jeffery made me go shoot every time he visited. Joan, you have a go." She pulled the target up and put a new one in.

Joan pulled the clip out, tried the action, and reloaded. She looked at Sister's target and said, "Hum." Jeffery and Elmore quietly walked up behind her as she eyed the target. Joan aimed and rapidly shot five in the center of the head, making one significant hole.

"Damn," said Jeffery. "I certainly can't beat that."

Elmore pulled the target in as the other men joined them. He looked at all three targets.

"Very nice shooting. This yours, Sister?" He held up the one with the five head shots.

"Of course it is," said Mary. "They have longer arms."

Arthur patted her shoulder, "That's right, and they're taller. Gives them a better perspective."

"See?" Mary said, as she stepped back and looked at the women.

Sister and Joan walked over and stood on either side of Mary and looked at the targets. Then they both looked down at Mary and put their arms around her. Joan then looked at the men, "That's why we've been designated as her security body people."

"Do any of you think you can do better?" Sister asked. "Like maybe go into ladies' rest rooms with her, or women's dressing rooms in stores?" She waited. Hearing nothing she said, "Can we move on to the new guns?"

Mary shrugged their arms off and rolled her eyes, "Oh boy, outshot and one-upped."

Romano went to the target and cleaned up the area. He then put a 3' x 3' metal upright behind the target so the bullets would fragment and fall. He laid down a cloth to catch the fragments of the next bullets. When he walked back he said, "These rounds are to just get you used to the guns, sights and feel. Use as few rounds as you need. Ladies first," he said as he handed Mary her gun.

Mary took the gun, looked it over, and asked Romano, "Is there much kick?"

"No, Mary, About the same as your Beretta; maybe a bit less. You'll notice it seems lighter and is a bit slimmer. Does it fit your hand?"

Mary fiddled about with the gun, aimed it and moved it about. Then fired off three shots, all into the head. "I like it. It shoots straighter than my old one. Here Joan, you try with mine. There are still a few left."

Joan took the gun hefted it, looked it over very carefully. "May I take it apart when we're done?"

"Sure, then you can clean it as well,"Mary answered with a smirk.

Joan lined it up and ripped off three shots, all in the same hole above the nose. Nodding she said, "Nice, I like it. I don't suppose I can get one, huh?"

Romano smiled and said, "Afraid not," he said as he handed Sister hers. She went through the same routine as Mary and Joan and did just as well. "Remember to clean it when we're done, and keep it safe." Sister nodded.

The men lined up using the same target. They all did well. They each picked a different spot on the target. When they were done, Romano went to the target area, took a broom and, with Jeffery's help, swept and bagged all the fragments.

When he came back Joan asked, "May I?" and reached for the bag. She took out a couple of the larger pieces and felt them. Then she took Mary's gun emptied out the last 2 bullets. "Hum. I don't suppose you're going to tell me what this material is, are you?"

Romano shook his head. He handed her Mary's bag and said, "The cleaning supplies are in here for both of Mary's guns. Don't mix them up." He stared at her, "I'm very serious."

Joan palmed the gun, rubbed the surface, "I'll just lust for it. I'll clean it Mary, both of them very carefully. Thank you for letting me fire it."

Romano and Jeffery put the metal pieces and the bag in the back of the wagon and packed up the guns just before the Sheriff returned. "Have fun?" the Sheriff asked as he walked up. "I won't ask why you needed to have this place so private. Ray guns, I bet. Romano, Elmore are you staying at the ranch or at Santoni's?"

"Santoni's. Mac and Sister are setting us up with the neighbors and the people we bought the ranch from to get it back in shape. What to plant, who to hire, should they live in, all sorts of stuff. Hate being absentee owners."

Elmore laughed, "Better than not being owners at all. Anyhow Mac and Sister will be sure whoever is hired will be good."

The Sheriff turned to Sister and Mary, "Did my wife call and say we would be delighted to come and have some New Year's Eve cheer with you?"

"Yes, she did," Mary said. "Sister said New Year's Eve at the vineyards was an old tradition. I'm glad we can keep it going. She didn't tell me what all it included. I think she's afraid to."

"I'll bet she is. You just wait, Mary. You'll meet half of Sonoma."

Sister put her arm around Mary's shoulder. "Don't listen to him! If it weren't for his wife, I'm not sure he would even get an invitation."

"Oh boy!" Arthur said when he put his arm around the Sheriff. "See what I suffer? One, a boss who just goes off and gets in trouble, and another, a Master who encourages her. Neither demonstrate any respect for our loyal police officers. It's a terrible…" he continued as the two men walked off laughing.

"Now Sister, it's time to tell me what to expect, what I'm to do, and, you know," she waved her hand in the air, "all that goes into entertaining half the countryside."

With Sister on one side with her arm through Mary's and Joan on the other, the three strolled off to the car. The men were joining Romano and Elmore to spend time at the ranch to discuss the future actions for the regeneration of the ranch and farm land.

Over lunch at Bodega, Sister explained that the parties were held at both Bodega and Twisted Hills, both catered. At Twisted Hills the children and parents of the workers and their relatives and friends gathered and had food and drink and dancing. They started a bit early because of the children.

At Bodega, the friends of Mac, the two managers, the Fosters, and Salinases gathered and ate and danced and drank. The Fosters and Salinases arrived a bit late and left early to rejoin the others at Twisted Hills. They were really hosting both, in a way. So were Mary, Mac, Arthur, and Sister.

The friends of Mac's included people from all walks of life in Sonoma and Napa. Mary had met many of them: Local officials, lawyers, teachers, other growers. Not more than a hundred, Mac always said, but sometimes it seemed more.

They had hams, turkeys, roasts, and all the trimmings set out. Small bands came to play at both places as well as off-duty cops to mind the traffic. The people arrived around eight thirty to nine, which gave Mary, Mac, and Sister time to go to Twisted Hills early to pay their respects, as that party started earlier. That band, like the food, had some spice added. None of their people were expected to work the party. It was for them. This had gone on for years.

The Twisted Hills party was less formal but still dressy in a different way. "You'll see," Sister told her. "I love them both and when the Fosters and Salinases leave to go to back to Twisted Hills, we won't see them again. We call it a night by one o'clock. Twisted Hills goes on longer. The children are bedded down in various houses and checked on by parents."

Mary listened carefully. "Good, then this is a tradition. Not just a Happy New Year, but a thanks for the old one?"

Sister looked at her and smiled. "You can say that. The families who owned Twisted Hills and the Bodegas go back a long way. When you bought Twisted Hills, I asked Arthur if we could continue this event. Mac had told him to deal with me. Barbara had just died. We were both a mess as was the staff. Hard as it was, it turned out to be a good thing. It helped with the healing for everyone. I know you haven't been here before for the holidays. You should find this interesting and fun. Yes, everyone dresses. For their safety we will keep the dogs in the house and the barn. If someone hits a fence, thats okay—but not an animal."

The next day, Saturday, went by fast. The weather was warm, and since the pool was heated, the kids and some adults went swimming. Jeffery told Mary that he, Romano, Sue, and Nancy were going out to dinner and dance. Toni was spending the night with friends. Sister told her she was having Joan down for dinner, and did Mary want to join them?

Mary said no, she was playing bridge with Mac, Arthur, and Elmore. Mac was grilling steaks. She suggested that Elmore and Romano spend the night again. Joan said she would ask Sister if she could spend the night with her at her place and let the boys have her room. Everyone seemed satisfied with the arrangements. Joan packed an overnight bag and left with Sister. Elmore was delighted to play bridge, especially when he found out Mary would be his partner. Romano told Arthur and Mac to watch that he didn't fleece them.

Sister built a fire in the living room fireplace, as the temperature had dropped with the sun. She did the steaks and baked potatoes. Joan set the table, made the salad, warmed the rolls and opened the wine Sister handed her. While they ate, they laughed, talked about the past days and the fun they had. After dinner and the dishes were done Sister said she had a new movie. The TV was near the fireplace, they both sank into the couch with glasses of port and saluted each other.

When the movie was over they were slumped down in the couch with their feet on the coffee table and holding hands. Joan looked at Sister, leaned into her, stroked her cheek and softly kissed her lips. She sat back, "Hum, that was nice. I've never done anything like that."

Sister said, "Yes it was, want to try again?"

Joan purred.

Chapter 13

Wednesday

Arthur and Mary were on the plane to Florida. Jeffery had stayed at Bodega to spend time with Manuel, learning how to prune grape vines. It was that time of the year, and pruning was not easy: It took time and guidance to do it right. Arthur said he had a bit of business in Florida he would see to, spend a day with Mary, and fly back to Bodega. He, too, was learning to prune. Then they would take Toni to Chicago with them so she could start graduate school the first of February.

Arthur told Toni she could stay with him till she found housing that suited her. His secretary was already looking into suitable housing. Romano and Elmore took Joan, Nancy and Sue to New York. They all teased that this flying around the country in private planes would ruin them for the future.

"Okay Arthur, what is this business you have to see to in Florida? Don't tell me it is to see me and the dogs home safely!"

"Ah Mary, my dear, of course it is." He paused and looked at her. "Not too believable huh?"

"No."

"Okay. I want to talk with Sheriff Gray about this trafficking business..." Mary started to interrupt, "No hear me out. I spoke with Santoni about this whole business of Pablo Galeano's death last summer in Sonoma and the trouble his father may be having with his son Diego. I told Santoni I'd had to share some of this with Sheriff Gray, not only because of you, but because that bastard Hudson lives in Ponte Vedra. The fact that he shot Pablo and saved lives was only to save his own neck. We told Sheriff Gray that then. If the son Diego takes it into his head to seek revenge, I want you protected. Mary, the more the Sheriff knows the better off you are."

Mary sat quietly and thought it over. She hated to have anyone know about her personal business. However the Sheriff had been involved with her, Jeffery and Arthur over several incidents in the past. She mentally shrugged and thought, 'what's one more?' "Arthur I don't want to look protective of Santoni and I know you told the Sheriff a bit about him and what happened last summer. How can you convey to Gray that Santoni, and especially Romano, and Elmore, are my friends, regardless of their occupations?"

Arthur leaned back and eyed Mary. "How delicately you put that. I mean you don't just come out and say the head of one of the largest crime syndicate in the world is my friend, now do you?"

"No, you don't, and you know damn well what I'm trying to say. I want him to hang that damn Hudson and forget about Santoni. How's that for clarity?"

"You know, my dear, Sheriff Gray is a very smart man and he knows you and Jeffery quite well. I'm sure this won't throw him off too much." Mary started to speak. "…No, say no more! The idea that Santoni wants to get rid of the trafficking and will do everything in his power to do so, will be just the entree we need. I have an appointment with him tomorrow. I think it is best if you are not involved at all. Is that okay?"

"Yes, Jeffery has taught me what I can and cannot get involved in. Curiosity has no place in many of his affairs." She paused. "However, I have learned that if I want to know badly enough, you will tell me. That's good enough for me.

"You know, Arthur, it's getting harder and harder to come back here. I never thought I would say that. I love Florida and my home here, but I now have a huge family back there. I miss them already."

"I know you do. I was watching you all day yesterday. You would look at them and then away. You are not losing any one, Mary. All of us have jobs to do, it just so happens these jobs are far apart. We're lucky we can all get together like we do. I think we just need to plan on doing so more often. Time is the only inconvenience we have. You'll see. It'll work out and get easier. By the way, did you pack your Beretta?"

"Yes. Why do you ask?"

"I saw you give your new gun to Joan for her trip. I'm glad you did. I just want to be sure you have the Beretta with you. I don't like that Taurus."

"Are you okay with Joan going to Europe with you and Mac?"

"Yes, she and Sister came to Mac and me. They told me they had asked you and you said it wasn't your trip.—they had to ask us."

"True."

"Mac and I were in immediate agreement. We both thought she would be an elegant addition to the group." He smiled.

"That's an interesting way to put it."

"It is, and pretty much the same general thing that Elmore and Romano said. The people we will be dealing with are mostly men. Sister will be introduced as the vineyard's Master, Joan as our consulting secretary." Before Mary could ask, Arthur went on to explain that that term covered a multitude of things.

"Elmore said these people we are visiting, although open enough to our visit and questions, will keep most of their knowledge about fine points of producing the best in Champagne and Port to themselves. We will, of course, ask many questions, as will Sister. Joan will listen and take notes on what they are 'not' saying out loud. She may direct a question to them but more likely tell one of us to."

"My God, is that ethical?"

"No more unethical than telling Santoni, of course his guests are welcome, and there will be no secrets." He couldn't help but grin. "The ladies did mention they would appreciate a stop in Paris for bit of window shopping. One day would do, they said. We thought we could do that just before we left for Portugal."

Mary rolled her eyes. "Those two are well suited. Sue said Joan told her when she and Sister were in San Francisco they shopped till they dropped. They like each other's company. I knew Joan rode but not dressage. It took a few times around the arena for her to get up to speed."

"Did Sister sit on the fence and give directions?"

"No, Joan asked her something about Sheba at the start. Sister told her she was a dancer. That's all it took. Sue said Joan was an only child of older parents. She was brought up with horses and tutors. She had a hard time till one of her tutors told her parents she was a telepath. Apparently the parents were knowledgeable and understanding. The tutor had a brother who was a telepath and a professor at one of the colleges. He and his sister spent time with Joan till she understood about her gift. Sue's parents were careful with her and her sister Babs as well. However, Sue had her sister and they worked out a lot between them.

"Joan was very bright and spent hours in her parents' library reading philosophy and history. She shot through college and graduate school. Got a dual P.D. in psychology and philosophy. Went to analytical school, started a practice in New York and hooked up with a group of psychics. Sue said Joan told her it was like finding a second family. Her parents are dead now, and Joan was left quite wealthy. She kept the home in Connecticut and the horses. Has a condo in the city and people who care for the horses and the property. Spends her weekends there. Has lot of friends but does not suffer fools gladly.

"Sue told me, when Joan first met me she thought I might be a long-lost sister. We fit together so well. The four of us—and now add Sister—are all quite close without having needed any time to get that way. I'm sorry, Arthur, does that make any sense?"

"Yes, Jeffery mentioned that one day. He said none of you needed any time at all getting to know each other. It seemed, he said, like a complete recognition, on contact. Is that the psychic stuff?"

"Some of it might be for Joan and Sue. When Babs was alive, she was an empath. She told me that Nancy and I were sensitives. She used words like perceptive, discerning, intuitive, tuned in quickly. She said we appeared to be watching others till we processed whatever it was that needed processing. I laughed. I told her I didn't believe anyone could ever be accused of calling me sensitive. She quickly corrected me and said there were two different meanings. She also made it clear that both Nancy and I, while being very amiable and congenial, kept our distance with most people. I think Sister is like that as well."

Arthur thought about that as he got up to get some coffee. He stood looking down at Mary. "Then when you all met each other, after only a bit of interaction, it all jelled, didn't it?"

"It certainly seemed that way. Each in a different way, under different circumstances, different times, of course, but I guess you could say the chemistry was the same."

"Did you ever talk about this to any of the others? I mean other than Babs?"

"No. Babs was different. Last summer when she, Sue, and I were walking on the beach at the Serenata Beach Club. We were in deep conversation about one of the psychics Babs was having trouble with, you know, the one who later killed her. Anyhow, when we joined the others they all remarked that the three of us looked and acted like sisters, especially from a distance.

Babs and Sue both said simultaneously, 'We are!' I laughed and said yes, after you remove some years.

"But Arthur, you know there was a kind of mind meshing, you could call it, between us. Something I know sisters often share. We laughed it off and hugged but it was very real. Maybe that is sort of like what you're seeing."

"Would you then say when you are not with them, I mean apart in distance, that this makes you miss them more?"

"Yes, I think you're right. Especially in the short term. Then one gets busy; it all evens out. I think what you saw in me yesterday was me anticipating the distancing that would come. Arthur, you are very good at this analysis."

"Mary, I love you. You are fascinating to me. You are never the same. You are a constant surprise. I'm a very lucky man to have someone who will never bore me."

Thursday morning, early

Mary dropped Arthur off at the Sheriff's office. He told her he would walk over to her office when he was done. Mary would take him to the St. Augustine airport, where his plane was, on her way home. She told him she only needed to show her face and collect her mail. She would then work at home.

When Arthur walked into Sheriff Gray's office, his assistant, Major Brown, was waiting with him. After the catch-up chatter, Arthur brought them up to date on what Santoni told him about Pablo Galeano's young brother Diego's desire for vengeance for Pablo's death. He also told him what Santoni and his friends were doing to search out and end trafficking. Before Sheriff Gray could say anything, he went on and suggested one should not look a gift horse in the mouth.

"Okay Arthur, I hear you. It's just a bit odd to be working with the enemy." He held his hand up, "When it comes to trafficking, I'll work with the devil himself to stop it. You say he will provide us with information?"

"Yes, but this is not a business that his people are involved in, so whatever he learns will be from others."

"Doesn't matter, it's the shipments into Florida that we need to catch and stop. Will he have someone set up a line of communication with me? As you know I'm part of the statewide group and I can send on whatever we get without anyone knowing where it came from."

"I'll tell him and help you all set up a communication system. You must know he is not any more interested in being associated with the authorities then you are with him. I think I can guarantee you will have a wall between you. Jeffery is aware of all this and may be of help if necessary."

"Oh boy," Said Major Brown. "How did he like that?"

"It's been a real adjustment. You know Santoni and two of his assistants bought land on the coast not far from Mary's vineyards. They all met last fall and became friends. They have a wall between business and pleasure. The younger men spent the holidays with us.

"This gets me to the second part of why I'm here. You know that 'bastard Hudson,' as Mary calls him, lives in Ponte Vedra. If Diego finds out he is the one who killed his brother, I fear he will be here like a shot. His father is worried and is watching him and keeping Santoni informed. They are old friends, almost like brothers. The father does not want his son killed nor does he want him to kill."

"Tricky. Mary knows all this, I assume?" Arthur nodded his head. "So it's okay if I talk with her? Not about the trafficking, but the brother?"

"Yes, I will call you immediately if word comes about the brother." He then went on and told him about his trip to Europe and the wine country. He also explained Mary's attitude concerning Santoni and his young assistants. "They treat her with great respect. She returns that respect. How he makes a living has nothing to do with their relationship. She has made that clear to Jeffery. He finally understands. He rather likes Romano, Elmore's assistant. I played bridge with Mary and Elmore, who were partners. You only want to hope those two never go into business together."

Chapter 14

Spain
Late January

Galeano's secretary rang his phone, "Excuse me sir, Mateo is here to see you."

Mateo was his right hand man and didn't need an appointment. There were men who screened everyone who came to see him before they got to his secretary. He had become more careful in recent years, especially since he went to war on the traffickers. The world was too big, too much money, too many players. He admitted he liked it all much better years ago.

"Come Mateo, sit. It is late in the day; would you like a glass of wine?"

"Thank you, sir. Don't get up, I can pour. One for you as well?"

"Yes, tell me you don't bear bad news."

Mateo poured two glasses of wine and sat down opposite Galeano. "Well, not bad news, but not good either. First, business: That is all good. We are making money, the vineyards have produced very well, arms sales are up, and money is moving smoothly. Miguel is doing very well. His studies in accounting and international finance have served him and us well. He's working with the auditors to tighten up the inventory. Also, he has reviewed the books from the vineyards. While he was doing, that he was told that Diego had been going over Pablo's books. Diego had asked the secretaries for all of Pablo's phone records for the past year, as well as all his expense records, and all the records for the company plane. He did not remove the records from the office, but made copies of some of them.

"Miguel said he told the secretary all these past records needed to be closed and not be made available to anyone else. If someone wanted them, they were to be referred to Mateo."

Galeano rubbed his face, took a swallow of his wine, and said, "He's on the hunt, isn't he?"

"It appears so. Miguel said the records showed Pablo's phone calls to America, to a man named Hudson in Florida, and one named Cesar Ruiz in California. I checked our records on both these men. Cesar Ruiz is a realtor who does business with syndicate men from all over the world. He covers the western and southwestern part of the United States and Mexico, even some parts of South America. Hudson is one of Galeano's gofers. He is low level, what we may call a runner."

"He was in California with Pablo. Wasn't he here last year, checking shipment business for Santoni? One of Santoni's men was with him."

"Yes, one of his top assistants, who is multilingual, was sent with him on his trips through the countries. Santoni wanted to be sure that Hudson was capable of doing the inventory and sales work. Hudson is an arrogant man who has good manners but an air of what I call an inflated sense of his worth. He acts like he has much more going for him than reality dictates. When he met Pablo, they became close—hero worship on Hudson's part and looking for a useful peon for Pablo. Bad combination, no possibility of check and balance. Pablo had both the money and knowledge of vineyards. Hudson seemed, I'm sure, a valuable friend to Pablo, who he thought was close to Santoni. It appears Pablo invited Hudson to go to California with him on vacation and on a buying trip for new vineyards. He had this Ruiz looking for vineyards for him."

"What did Santoni tell you about the shooting? Did he say who all was involved?" asked Mateo.

"Only that he knew the vineyard owners and was having dinner with them and their friends when Pablo burst into the room with Hudson and got the drop on both the owner's financier and on Santoni. He said Pablo took Hudson by surprise, but he went along and held a gun on Santoni. At the last minute when Pablo was yelling at Hudson to shoot Santoni, Hudson turned his gun on Pablo."

"Was Santoni trying to buy these people's vineyards?"

"No, he was in the process of buying acreage over on the coast. The past owner of the vineyards was helping him with the sale. Nothing at all to do with vineyards."

"How did Pablo come to the conclusion that they were trying to steal the vineyards from him?" Mateo was a detail man and didn't hesitate to ask questions.

"I'm not sure. I was told Hudson was, what they call a 'basket case.' He kept saying over and over that Pablo went nuts. Let me talk with Santoni and get more information from him. Also, I'll ask him about this Ruiz man. Keep an eye on Diego. I know he has many interests, but I don't want him leaving the country."

After Mateo left, Galeano looked at his watch. Just after six in London. Maybe Santoni would still be in the office. Santoni's secretary said, "Hello, Mr. Galeano. How can I help you?"

"Well, for starters you could consider coming to Spain and working for me."

"How lovely. However, I'm sure Mr. Santoni would not approve that move. Let me ring him for you."

"Yes, my friend," said Santoni. "Is it wine time already? If you'll wait, I'll pour myself a glass." After a brief pause, he said, "How can I be of help to you? Or is it just a need to spend the end of the day with an old friend?"

"Both. Mateo just left. He gave me an update on my son Diego— one I'm not very happy with. Let me tell you what he reported and what information I hope you can fill in for me." He went on and recited all that Mateo had said.

"I would like to know more about this Ruiz and what is happening to him now. What did he have to do with my son? What was his role in all this mess?"

Santoni thought, I knew this day would come but not quite in this way. He knew Galeano was a brilliant business man. He ran a huge wine business from the growing to the selling as if it were a sideline to the business of the cartel. Not many men could accomplish one, much less both. "I will tell you as much as I know at this point. Ruiz is in the business of buying and selling land and businesses of every sort. He has many customers. Many are in our business. He acts as the middle man finding the property and helping in the early negotiations. He has a reputation of being able to match buyer to seller without complications."

"Have you ever done business with him?"

"No, my friend, if I want to buy something, especially as important as a vineyard or property, I go to the owner directly. I don't believe in wasting money on go-betweens. I did check on him and several of the people in our business have used him. He is helpful for those who are in the speculatively business. He is known to be competent and honest with his clients.

"I understand from the past owner of the Bodega Vineyard that Ruiz had tried to approach him a number of times but the owner had put him off. Told him he wasn't interested. Apparently Ruiz then went to the neighboring vineyard, Twisted Hills. It had been sold a few years before but he tried them, with the same results. What he didn't know was that the new owner of Twisted Hills had been approached by the owner of Bodega Vineyards to buy his vineyard. They were in the process of closing on that sale when Ruiz showed up.

"Apparently Ruiz tried to explain to Pablo that neither vineyard was for sale. Pablo would not take no for an answer and when he got to California he went to the new owner and suggested that he buy into both the vineyards. He also had Ruiz stage an auto accident on the owner of the vineyards. She was an expert driver and escaped without injury.

"A few days later, when he went to the Bodega Vineyard for a tasting, he discovered they also had dressage horses. While he was there, Hudson was with him, and recognized my men who were there riding. They were there because I was buying property on the coast, and the late owner of Bodega was helping me. He still lived at Bodega as a consultant. My men had been invited to ride.

"Later that day, there was an attempted attack on the new Bodega's owner while she was in the field grading the grapes. The assailant escaped."

"Later, it was revealed, Pablo thought with her out of the way both vineyards would have to be sold. He failed. He scared Hudson, who now wanted to go back to Florida that night but Pablo talked him into staying till morning. They went to a fancy restaurant in the hills for dinner. Unfortunately it was the same place I, with the owners and some of their friends, was having a celebratory dinner over my purchase of the land on the coast.

"I told you what later happened. When it was over, Hudson told the police that when Pablo saw us all together in the restaurant he just flipped out. He was convinced I was buying the Vineyards and everyone was lying to him. He waited a while and then came into the private room where our party was dining. He surprised us, held us all at gun point, and told us what he believed. Also he said he was going to kill me and the vineyards owners. He was raving. He demanded that Hudson shoot me. I don't know what made Hudson shoot him. Some sort of sanity and fear for himself made him act. If he hadn't it would have been a massacre. I want you to know, I do not believe Hudson was acting any way but out of selfish fear for himself. He is not an honorable man. I have him back in Florida at his home. I have not decided what to do about him."

Galeano was silent, and Santoni honored that silence. He knew his old friend and how much pain he was in, he only hoped this telling would help him understand, if not heal.

"Pablo loved his horses. He had some of the best dressage horses in Spain. He must have thought he had discovered a second paradise. One he could own and control on his own, not something of his father's. Owned by a mere woman who knew nothing of wine or horses. He thought it should be his, it was meant to be his." He was quiet a moment.

"Santoni, my friend, I'm sorry all this happened. Thank you for telling me. I know now you could not have told me before. It is not a story a man wants to hear about his son. It would have been a greater tragedy had it not been stopped. I would have lost not only a son but my best friend."

"Thank you. Now what is bothering you about Diego?"

"He is searching through all of Pablo's records. He believes that Pablo was cheated out of the vineyards. He believes when Pablo found out and approached them, they killed him. He thinks this Hudson who works for you was part of it. I know he is making all this up, but I don't know how to stop this kind of thinking. I have my men watching him. If he makes a move to leave the country I will call you immediately. Now, what have you found out about trafficking in the US?"

Santoni gave him a rundown on what he found out. He told him he was keeping track of it through friends. He would have no direct contact with the authorities. He told Galeano that he would tell him everything he hears. He also told him he wanted to alert one of his friends in the states about the possibility of Diego seeking vengeance for Pablo's death. He did not want them to be taken by surprise. Galeano expressed his sadness that this seemed necessary but he agreed that they should be alert. He repeated that he would keep a close watch on his son.

Santoni sat at his desk and thought about the call. Not wanting to repeat himself, he asked his secretary to get both Romano and Elmore for him and then go home.

When they arrived he asked them to sit, and poured them a glass of wine and told them about his conversation with Galeano. He said, "I want to call Arthur and alert him to the situation. I am going to suggest he tell all the others to exercise caution. Especially if they notice any strange men hanging about." There was silence. "Well?" he said.

Elmore looked thoughtful. "I'm wondering if there is a different way we could put that."

Santoni laughed. "Yes, they are all good looking women. Having a strange man paying attention to them would not be unusual."

Romano smiled, "We have a picture of Diego. We have pictures of everyone who has anything to do with the business. Lets send that to Arthur and ask him to share. I really think that would be helpful."

"I agree, Romano. Get the best one. It must be clear."

Elmore laughed, "I heard Diego is a very handsome young man. I can just hear the ladies having a good laugh. Saying, 'Be a shame to shoot such a hulk.' I can hear it now."

Santoni smiled. He had spent time with them. Even knowing they might be in danger, he believed they would laugh. Wonderful accomplished women, who seemed to have lived lives that enhanced their sense of self and therefore their ability to live life completely and not fear the unknown, at least not unnecessarily. Those traits helped explain how they got together as friends. Likes attract, he believed. Now he needed to bring a bit of forewarning into their lives.

Chapter 15

January
Early Afternoon

"Great lunch Arthur. I enjoyed talking with Toni. She seems to have settled in that lovely apartment building for graduate students. I'm glad she invited us to lunch with her friends and roommate."

"Yes, Jeffery, I agree. My secretary helped her get started on her search, then she just went with what her gut told her was right. These young ones have wonderful antennae for each other. My secretary told me they seek out those like them. That graduate building caters to graduate students from out of town, so they're all starting on a similar footing."

The phone on his desk buzzed. "Yes, Rose?"

"Mr. Santoni, in London."

"Hello Oliver. Are you ready for our arrival?"

"Certainly! In a week, I believe. I'm glad you can stay overnight and have dinner with us."

"It will have to be an early night. Elmore told me we leave just before dawn for our before-noon appointment at the first vineyard. He thought the first day we could get an overview and then the next day or two focus on areas we may want to know more about. He said he built some flexibility in with the vineyards. I'm glad he also made it possible with the hotels for them to adjust to our schedule."

"Yes, he knows these people. They have mutual respect. I have Romano and Elmore with me. We have some information to share."

"Jeffery is here with me. Is that okay with you?"

"Yes, it will save time and offer us a chance to seek out the best advice."

Jeffery grinned, "Yes, I'm it."

"Oh boy," said Romano. "Never give him an opening." Ever since Christmas, Jeffery and Romano had established a sort of camaraderie. It made Elmore and Arthur smile, and Santoni liked to hear it without knowing how it came about.

Santoni cleared his throat, which brought the two into line. "My friend Galeano called today. He is very worried about his son Diego. He's had his men following all Diego's movements. Mateo, his senior man, reported to him that his assistant, Miguel, found that Diego had been going over Pablo's personal books and records. Galeano said this tells him that Diego is on the hunt. Apparently Miguel is well educated and has been going over the vineyard accounts, and thats how he discovered Diego's activities. Galeano had told Mateo to keep careful track of his sons activities."

"Mr. Santoni," said Romano, "This man Miguel was at University when I was. He is very sharp. He is also a dressage rider. If there was something out of line, he would report it immediately. Elmore and I also know Mateo. They had to be deeply worried if they brought this to Galeano's attention."

"Yes, I know," Santoni replied. "Galeano trusts his senior men, as do I. Galeano asked for more specifics about Pablo's behavior and relationships in California. I related everything you told me and what I already knew. We have known each other many years and he would know if I hedged anything. He was appalled at Pablo's behavior and made no attempt to excuse any of it.

"He desperately wants to stop Diego from his persistent belief that the vineyard people and Santoni were trying to steal from Pablo, and then murdered him. He will not listen to his father. He has been avoiding him as much as he can. He knows Diego is partying and may even be using drugs. Diego does not know Miguel personally. He may have seen him around, but they feel it's safe for Miguel to observe him in the bars and other social places."

Arthur was quiet and pensive. Jeffery was on his feet pacing around the room. He stared out the windows. Turning, he looked at Arthur. "We can't lock her up can we?" Arthur smiled at that remark.

Santoni listening, smiled, as did Romano and Elmore, when they heard Arthur say, "Like trying to put a cat in a bag."

"Wouldn't want to be the one holding that bag." Elmore said with a smile.

"It's all right for you guys to laugh. She's alone in Florida." He paused as Arthur interrupted him.

"Jeffery, when I was there last month I had a meeting with the Sheriff. I told him there may be a problem with the brother. He said he would talk with Mary about this. He is also agreeable to working with us on the trafficking. I'll call him and bring him up to date on the brother, after I call Mary."

"Hi, Arthur. It's early in the day to have the pleasure of a call from you." Mary eased back in her desk chair. She was at home working her way through a thick DRI request. These plans for development of regional impact were long, and could be tedious. Mary had learned the hard way of the necessity of reading each page and making notes on what she didn't understand. She had been reading these things for a long time as a citizen activist. She knew how easy it was for a developer to slip something in, hoping the citizens wouldn't see it, or the staff just skip over it unless it was a major infraction of the rules.

"Hi, yourself. How come you're home in the middle of the day?"

"No meetings, and I told my secretary to take messages and when I take a break I'd call her." She went on to tell him about the DRI she was reviewing. It was a bad one, she told him, which made it even more necessary that she read it carefully. "I'm only half through and I already have three pages of notes. Now what is so major you are calling in the middle of your day?"

Arthur explained that Jeffery was in the office with him and would be on the speaker phone. He explain Santoni's call. He said he was notifying everyone and sending two pictures of Diego to everyone and to the sheriff. He personally wasn't concerned at the moment since Diego was still at home in Spain. He told her that his father, Galeano, had his son being watched by his senior men.

"Mary, Galeano is a very old and close friend of Santoni. He is also deeply involved in shutting down trafficking in Spain and everywhere he can. He took this and his late son Pablo's part in it as a personal affront to the honor of his family."

"Old World standards: It's nice to see they still matter. However, Arthur, as long as Diego remains in Spain, I think I'm going to be fine."

"See? I told you she would ignore us." Jeffery said.

"Jeffery." Arthur said.

"No, don't you Jeffery me. Mary, you must take this seriously. I listened to Santoni. He certainly is taking it seriously."

"Oh! Is he sending me bodyguards?" She heard Arthur try to cover a laugh.

"God, I told you she wouldn't listen."

"Excuse me, Jeffery, I am listening. What is it you want me to do? Go into hiding somewhere, and if so for how long?"

"I…"

"Never mind." Mary interrupted him. "I have my gun and, at home, my dogs. I am surrounded by people all day. Granted, some of them are not too fond of me, but bodily harm is not on my horizon. In case you are thinking of coming down here and watching my every move, forget it. I'd love to have your company and if it wasn't so damn cold out we could go fishing. Instead I suggest you continue your lessons in grapevine trimming."

There was silence on the phones. Mary heard a door slam. "Mary," said Arthur, "you were a little hard on him, you know."

"I know, however, he is developing a tendency to hover. He always was protective but last summer set him off."

"Don't forget, Mary, he had to sit at a table and watch you almost get killed. That is, after you were almost run off the road and an attempt made on your life in your own vineyard. It does tend to sharpen the senses, you know."

"I…"

Arthur interrupted, "Plus, he has acquired more people he cares deeply about than he ever had in his life. Not to mention a growing friendship with one of a syndicate man's top assistants. I must say, for a 'sensitive,' you are missing some serious signs. He's been on Overload and unlike his freelance work with criminals around the world, he can walk away from that when they are apprehended. With us, and you in particular, there is no walking away. You may not have wanted a son but you have one."

They were quiet for a while. "Hum. I guess the 'sensitive' label as a noun is not related to personal insight. There is something in the literature about knowing thyself. Arthur, I hope I have not hurt his feelings too much."

"I don't think so. Elmore and Romano were teasing about you not being too conducive to close oversight. He was warned. You are not a subject he can stand off from and analyze. I'll be calling the

Sheriff and sending him a picture of Diego, so don't be surprised when he calls you."

"Will they let you know if this man, Diego leaves Spain?"

"Yes, and probably you as well."

"What role has Hudson in all this? I mean, since Diego knows about the shooting of Pablo, surely he knows it was Hudson who shot him. Doesn't he?"

"Mary, Galeano knows about Hudson. He told Diego that Hudson shot Pablo to keep him from killing Santoni. Galeano doesn't know if he believes him. Diego has this idea in his head that the owner of the Vineyards and Santoni killed Pablo to keep him from getting the vineyards. It seems his father cannot talk reason to him. Diego worshiped Pablo and will hear nothing bad about him.

"Romano thinks that Diego may be crazy with grief. So there is no way they will be able to reason with him. Therefore, no one knows what he is thinking or what he will do. He's gotten this idea stuck in his head that they killed Pablo for the vineyards and has shut out everyone."

"So if he comes to Florida he might just be going after Hudson? Right?"

Arthur was silent. "Oh, boy," said Mary, "talk about wishful thinking. I guess I can't really hope to get rid of Hudson that way. Okay, tell me, are you all still scheduled to go to Europe next week?"

"Yes, Santoni and I were talking about that. We will go to London have an early dinner with him, Elmore, and Romano, and leave at dawn for France. I talked with Sister and Mac. They are excited to be off. We will meet Joan, Mac and Sister in New York, have dinner, then be off early to London. You know, Mary, despite this mess with Diego I'm really looking forward to this trip, especially with Mac and Sister, our experts. It should be exciting."

"How about Joan? Will she fit in? I mean she is not a wine maven."

"No, not a wine maven, but Elmore told me, with Joan and our proper questioning, we should get all the information we need. Between the four of us, if we can't learn how to make champagne, we shouldn't do it."

"You're told me Joan will listen to what they are not saying out loud?"

"Well, yeah. She discussed it with Elmore and Romano. They said these vineyard owners are beholden to Santoni and said they would tell us everything we need to know. Elmore said it would never happen. They will think we are just dumb Americans, so we will go after what we want another way. Actually, I think Elmore, Sister, Mac, and Joan are looking forward to the secret search."

"Oh, boy. One part of me wishes I was with you. Another says, no girl, you would do something to blow the whole thing. I hear the excitement in your voice. I'm so glad the four of you are going."

"Good. I'm going to call the Sheriff now, Jeffery is having dinner with me. I'll call you later."

Chapter 16

London
Sunday, Early February

"Smooth flight, Arthur?" asked Mac as he unbuckled and stood.

"Yes, it was. Santoni is sending someone to pick us up. We'll meet him, Elmore, and Romano at a country place of his firm. He said it's about a half-hour drive. We'll spend the night there and be off at dawn for a quick flight to France and our first stop. We have a rental car waiting for us in France, so I can let these guys go back to the States till we are done in Portugal."

"Isn't Elmore coming with us?" asked Sister.

"Yes, he'll fly down with us in the morning. When we are done in France, Romano will fly in, pick us up and take us to Portugal. Elmore will return to London. I didn't have to make the arrangements, Elmore made them all, including the cars and hotels. Europe is like their back yard. I never argue with the experts." He had told the pilots there was a hotel at the airport and room reservations had been made for them. They had an arranged departure time for the morning.

As they settled in the limo, Joan said, "Dress for dinner, I suppose."

"I'd think that would please Santoni," grinned Arthur. "Did you pack enough?"

"Arthur," Sister said. "Joan and I are seasoned travelers. Three styles or sets, one for running around the vineyards, one for shopping, and one for lovely dinners. All have interchangeable parts. Remember we are stopping in Paris between vineyards: We may add a few things."

"That goes without saying," added Joan. "We may even find something for Mary. We'll tell her it was from you."

Mac laughed. "Arthur, give it up. I've traveled with Sister, she has met her match with Joan. They will be dressed perfectly all the time and you will never understand where they kept it all. Mary told me Joan will be in heaven having her own plane to haul it all home in."

Arthur glanced at them as they nodded in unison. "So lovely," Joan murmured.

Half and hour later the limo drove through tall gates and down a long drive to a large stone house set in a wooded setting. The driver opened the car doors and a tall, well-built man came down the steps from the house and greeted them. He said, "My name is James, I will show you to your rooms. Mr. Santoni is on the way. Drinks would be in the library in about 45 minutes." It became obvious he did not deal in small talk. Not your typical English butler. They followed him up a sweeping staircase and down a wide hall.

James opened a door. "This is one of our larger suites." He walked in and across a lovely room and opened another door. "Through here is an adjoining room. They have separate bathrooms." He put Joan's luggage down and carried Sister's into the second room. He bowed his way out and quietly shut the door. Joan turned to Sister, and started to speak. Sister put her finger to her lips, "Let me freshen up. I think a short black sheath will be fine, don't you?"

Joan looked at her. "Yes, that sounds fine. We are beautiful in black. It was a hit in San Francisco. Let me see your room. Is it as lovely?" Joan put her arm around Sister's shoulder as they walked into the adjoining room. Joan bumped into her and whispered. "Talk to me in your head."

Sister thought, *"Arthur said this was a country place of the firm's. I bet it is wired for sound and visual."*

"Oh," Joan said. "Isn't this lovely? Elmore said it was a country place of the firm's, not a private home. I bet they have businessmen from all over the world staying here. Under the circumstances, I hope they have instructed James to turn off the audio and visual in these rooms—and especially in the baths."

Sister grinned at Joan. "There's a phone in this room. Let's call Santoni now, and be sure we have privacy, so we won't be late for drinks." Just then the phone rang. "Hello," Sister said.

"Your privacy is guaranteed in this entire suite. There is no need to bother Mr. Santoni. It is guaranteed throughout the house."

"Thank you James, I will tell Mr. Santoni of your thoughtfulness." The line went dead.

"That was quick." Joan said. "I think we should keep our secrets to ourselves though, till we get on the plane for France." She laughed and gave Sister a hug.

A short time later they descended the stairs, Elmore was waiting at the foot. He was grinning, "I hope you found everything you need. You arrived before us, so James hadn't been told you were family."

Sister and Joan put their arms through Elmore's as he lead them to the library. "It wasn't a problem. A small oversight, quickly corrected."

"Yes, quite quickly. James almost had a heart attack when you mentioned calling Santoni." Elmore looked at them with an eyebrow lifted. "He's not used to someone saying they will call Santoni to complain."

"Pity," Joan said. "He's not to worry—we won't be here long. We won't mention it to Santoni, you can set his mind at rest."

The library was a warm welcoming room. Not large in comparison to the rest of the house. Lined with book shelves. The center was composed of couches and chairs that asked you to come recline, read, or dream, complemented with a fireplace quietly adding warmth. The men all rose when Joan and Sister entered. Santoni gave both women a hug, as did Romano. "I'm so glad to see you. I'm almost tempted to go with you, especially to Portugal. I love port and the country. I was just asking Mac and Arthur what you hope to learn from the French." He smiled. "Sister, will you charm secrets from them?"

Sister smiled at Santoni. She truly did like the man. "I'm not sure what we will learn. I have read as much as I can about the production of champagne and port. Champagne's process is much more complex. The blending of three base wines to get the proper taste before you even get to the bottling and adding of the final ingredients."

"I agree," Mac said. "They have shortened the mechanical process, but you will need to be a tasting genius in the blending."

"Elmore has been reading as well. He told me Krug may use reserve vintages from six years ago." Romano said. "I asked him, how do they know what to use and how much?"

"Like Mac said, it takes a tasting genius, years of practice. I really look forward to asking and listening." Sister remarked.

"I think Sister will have an edge on me," Mac said. "Even if I have been growing and making wine all my life, I haven't had the education of a Master. They work on their ability to taste and distinguish even the most subtle of changes. Sister can tell you not only the grape, but where it came from, even perhaps who picked it. I count on her in the assemblage stage."

"What is that?" asked Santoni.

"It is the mixing of the various base wines together." Sister answered. "I read that they may have several members of the wine house asked to taste before it is complete. It is very detailed."

"Will they answer your questions?"

"I'm hoping they will. I'll be interested in how they know when enough is enough."

Joan laughed, "That's why they have me along." She raised her eyebrows at Santoni.

He stared at her, then burst into a smile. "Yes, you will hear them thinking about what to answer, if at all. Then what will you do, Joan? Ask a leading question?"

"Or, maybe a really dumb one. Just enough to give Sister a direction in which to go. I have read, but not enough to know what they will be talking about when they get into the fine art of blend and taste. However, Sister's answer to me may let them think some more, or even offer to help her. We'll see."

"You know, they may be more forthcoming than you expect. You are both very attractive women; they are French. They may find you so lovely and enticing they will just go ahead and tell you what you want to know, thinking it will do no harm—after all, you are only women," Romano said, grinning.

Joan eyed him. "Now wait, I meant that in strategic way."

"I know you did, dear. Just don't forget."

"So Sister, this tasting is not like a tasting of wine at your vineyards that people come to buy?"

"No, here they are tasting the base wines. Nothing has been added. No sugar or yeast. You would not find it appealing. Once they have found a mixture that is a proper blend for them then they go into the rest of the mixing of sugar and yeast. They have generations of experience behind them. Also, each year's grapes bring something new. We look for it as well with your new grapes, but in the champagnes you have three or more wines to taste, then blend,"

"Is the making of port as complicated?" Asked Santoni.

"Yes, and no," replied Sister.

"They no longer crush the grapes by stomping on them. It is all mechanized now. They let it rest for a day or so then add the spirit wine to interrupt the fermentation process. I don't know how they determine how long before they add the spirit wine, or how much they add. The end product is about nineteen to twenty percent alcohol. They are aged in wood for a time and then using various methods of filtration they are bottled. The wood aging varies. I don't now how they determine how long, or if they mix wines before bottling. So, you see, I have many questions."

"Mac, you too have questions?"

"Yes, don't let Sister fool you. We both have spent time with champagne and port makers in California so we are not going in totally ignorant. It is the subtlety of the timing, knowing when to stop the fermentation, when to bottle. A question of tasting, like with the champagne mixing of base wines, what grapes they use. I am hoping to get them to tell me what they think of our cabernet and chardonnay. These will be our major base wine grapes. For the champagne we will need pinot noir and even maybe pinot meunier grapes. We can buy those grapes to start."

"Okay, I give up. You two have spent your lives growing grapes and making wine. Arthur, you are well on your way to learning this business as well, it seems."

"I have always had a love of wines, and the chance to grow and make wines has been a great gift. Mary loves her red wines. She loves to grow things. This past summer, she began learning how to grade the ripeness of the grapes. Our vintner thought she would tire and/or get bored going up and down the rows, but these are her grapes, her babies; like her flowers, plants, and dogs. She used to drink store bought jug wine at home. Not anymore. She has only her own label now."

"Yes, she is something with the things that belong to her," Sister said. "She told me the horses were mine as much as hers. I see her out walking with them in the pasture. She talks with them and brings them treats. The follow her around like the dogs. She loves her friends equally as well, yet she maintains a certain distance. Not cold mind you, more like a respect for your space." Sister stopped but was nodding her head in agreement with what she had said.

"She showed no desire to come with us." Arthur said. "I think it would bore her to tears."

"It's like her shopping for clothes." Joan said. "She would wear rags, yet she knows good clothes and has great taste. She wears them well, but shopping for them is like pulling teeth. Nancy has known her the longest and she said it has always been like that. She doesn't care what she wears nor does she care what you wear. For a clothes horse like me it is a mystery. Last summer we girls went shopping. We picked outfits for her, had the stores put them away. The next day we went with her. She tried them on and bought almost everything we suggested. If we got just a bit off her style she would smile and set it aside."

Sister smiled. "Shopping for her for Christmas was a snap. I picked up some things Arthur mentioned and something from me. It was easy. She has excellent taste. I also found out she can buy for us easily. She is a jewel that needs protecting… and speaking of protecting, how is that family in Spain?"

Santoni nodded. "I spoke with Galeano yesterday. He said his son Diego seems to have settled down. He worshiped his brother Pablo. His brothers and sisters not so much. Galeano's men are watching him closely. He was keeping some bad company and drinking but that seems to have stopped. Let's hope it's all part of the grieving process, mixed in with hot Spanish temper." He stood as James stepped to the door. "Dinner is ready, it seems."

Santoni seated the women on each side of him, smiled at Arthur and Mac, "This is what is called the host's privilege."

Chapter 17

France
Early Monday morning

T hey landed at a private airport just north of Paris. Elmore told them they would be staying at a private house just north of the city on the road to Reims. The owners also owned a lovely restaurant they would dine at that night. They would pick up a car there. The first stop would be Krug's, and their renowned vineyard Clos du Mesnil. They would start with the blanc de blancs which are made with that vineyard's chardonnay grapes only. Krug makes only a small amount of this champagne. They have a big operation for their other blended grapes. They were most open to showing them both the blending process, Elmore explained

"Sister, I knew you would like to see how they deal with this particular champagne, since you grow such wonderful chardonnay grapes. The head vintner will be our guide, and as the day goes on, you and he can decide what you most want, and what Mac and Arthur want to learn."

They spent time touring the facility, discussing the whole process of making champagne from the type of grapes they used through the bottling. Sister told the vintner what she wanted while Arthur and Mac spun off to the areas of the casks and storage. Sister asked Andre, the vintner who did the primary work on the blancs, if he would take her through that process. She explained that she raised prize chardonnay grapes, and would, if possible, like to use those alone and do blanc de blancs. He agreed and they spent more time in that area. Sister asked if one could tell from sampling a chardonnay if it would make a good blanc de blanc. Joan heard him say in his head, 'Yes, any fool could tell a good grape, but our grapes are not just good.'

Before he could answer Sister, Joan asked if the grapes they used in the blanc could also be used in just a chardonnay wine. She smiled, "Andre, I mean, have you a bottle of chardonnay like that?

One that has not been made into a champagne?"

"We don't use these grapes for just a chardonnay wine, but," he tipped his head and shyly smiled, "I have made up a few for my own use. Why do you ask?"

"Well," Joan said, "I am not a Master, like Sister here," she nodded at Sister, "but Sister is making an award-winning chardonnay wine and I wonder if you could tell if it was good enough to use for your blanc de blanc champagne?"

Sister thought, 'Joan you are a tricky one, that is not why we are here—to see if mine is as good as theirs, even if I would love to know.' "I'm sorry, Joan is really not..."

He interrupted Sister. "No, it is a good question. Do you have a bottle with you?" Thinking, 'She is lovely, if ignorant. I will humor her.'

"We have some in the auto. Elmore said it would be good to bring our best as a gift for you. I'll run get it and we can try." She smiled into his eyes, as she stroked his arm. "Would you like?"

He was actually blushing as he looked at Sister and then back at Joan. "Yes, very good, we can sit and sip a bit. Come, Sister, I'll find a bottle of ours while Joan goes to her car."

Sister rolled her eyes after Joan as she hurried off. She and Andre sat and chatted about the making of champagne while he uncorked a bottle of chardonnay and set out some crackers.

He told her he was going to do the assemblage, "Blending you know, of some base wines in the morning. Would you like to come?" Sister beamed, said she would consider it a privilege to be asked to join him. He bent his head a bit and said, "Joan is, of course, welcome." The staff would be green with envy to see him surrounded by such beauty.

Joan strode in and Sister noticed Elmore trailing far in her wake. She was about to speak and he shook his head. "Here, Sister. It's yours to open."

Sister carefully opened the wine. It was one of their reserves. She poured a bit in a glass looked at it, swilled it, and tasted. She smiled and poured a bit into two clean glass and handed one to the Andre the other to Joan. He carefully went through the process of tasting. Looked puzzled. Tasted again and reached, taking the bottle from

Sister. "Five years old. One of your first, I believe you said."

"Yes, the newer ones taste much the same. The grapes have held nicely. We won top awards this year. It's a Sonoma Valley wine."

The vintner set the glass down, ignored Joan and, picking up his bottle, he poured his wine into three new glasses, handing one to each of them. "Taste!" he commanded.

Sister smelled and tasted. "Lovely, just lovely. My god, no wonder your blanc de blancs are world renowned."

"Yes," he nodded. He took Sister's wine again and drank and nodded. Then his wine. "These grapes must have emigrated with one of my forefathers. This is wonderful. They are in the same family. I never would have believed it. When you go home, will you go and talk with the grower where you got the cuttings for these grapes? See if he knows of their origin."

"I will be delighted to seek him out and find where he thinks they came from. His is an old family."

"Yes, yes. See if they are in a separate area from the rest of his crop, and why he sold you these. Did he say they were separate and/ or different from others?"

Sister thought back. "I remember walking his land. I was looking for an area similar to where I wanted to plant his grapes on our land, a similar terroir. I didn't want to disturb them more than necessary. I remember when I suggested the ones I wanted, he smiled and said they were a good grape. A bit different than the others, but very good. I believe he sold his grapes mixed together to local wine makers." Sister sat and thought, smiled and looked at Andre, "I believe, when I return home, I'll go visit him and make a bid on that section of his grapes for next year."

"But, Sister won't he charge you more since your chardonnay has done so well?"

"He may, Andre, but I believe he will just add it up to the fact that our grapes all make wonderful wines. These growers know it's the vintner who determines the excellence of the wines." She looked at Andre with one eyebrow raised, "Isn't that so?"

"Yes, for the most part. There is no sense disbursing him of that thought. Let me go over the process of making this blanc de blanc champagne with you one more time. Joan, can you take notes for

Sister?"

"Yes, that's why I'm here."

He went over the process very carefully. The fermentation, the timing, the adding of the sugar, and the rest—how long he leaves them in the cask, then the bottling and on and on. Sister asked a few well-placed questions when he stopped. He said tomorrow he would expect them to be with him at the blending of the other champagnes. When they finished Elmore walked up and soon Mac and Arthur joined them. They finished the wine and crackers and sampling, and comparing the two wines.

Once they were in the car and on the way, Joan was almost bouncing up and down. "Can I tell them? Can I, Sister?"

Sister reached over and squeezed her hand. "Yes, they will never tell anyone."

Joan told them the whole story, and the wonderful end about how he was going to take them through the blending of the other grapes tomorrow. The tasting of the two chardonnays and the comparison intrigued Mac.

"Sister, they really are that similar?" Mac asked.

"Oh yes. When he opened his, he made me taste both. A mother and her lovely daughter. One as beautiful as they other. I was as astonished as he was. I told him I was going to bid on this man's grapes from that one section for the coming year."

Arthur eyed her, "You want to keep your prize chardonnay and do the champagne as well. How clever! What will people say when you succeed is producing a champagne blanc de blanc to rival Kurg's?"

"Oh what a lovely thought! Arthur, it would be a miracle. I would phone Andre and give him all the credit. I will also research where these grapes came from. Mac, you can help me with that. Your family goes back a long way, and we have a great vine historical society."

"Yes, I was thinking that. When you go out to talk with the grower about buying next year's crop, I'd like to go along." Sister held up her hand. "No, no, Sister! I will give him no cause to up his price. I do want to see his vineyards and where the other grapes grow. We will discuss the cultivation of all his grapes."

"Sister" asked Joan. "Can you tell, by taste, one grape from another if they are both Chardonnays?"

"Good question Joan. I'm sure in this case we'll be able to. Why don't you ask him tomorrow?"

"No, no. I don't know enough," she stopped and thought. "Hum, yes I will. It's just the kind of question he might expect from me. Never from you. Maybe he will do a show and tell with me." She eyed Elmore and rubbed his arm, "I just bet he would love to."

They all roared with laughter.

Tuesday

The next morning, everyone went to the Krug buildings where the other champagnes were made. It was a big operation. It was explained that the base wines had been made over the winter and the blending was just beginning. They used chardonnays, pinot noir and pinot meunier.

He said the chardonnay contributed finesse and elegance; pinot noir body and texture: and pinot meunier fruitiness and earth. These are not used in equal amounts. We use more chardonnay and pinot noir than meunier. We keep the base wine in casks. When we have the best blend from these we add sugar and yeast, and bottle. The tasting assessment and bench blending is going on now.

"I will do my best to explain, in English, as we go. I will have you taste as well. I'll tell you what I think it may need more or less of."

Sister kept up with him and asked a few questions. Joan, after a taste or two, stopped, as did Arthur, then Mac. "The base is high in acid, low in alcohol, its taste is rather meager. The makers blend these bases with an idea, a notion, and imagine what it will taste like in years to come. Any minor fault in a base wine may be amplified by the sparkling-making process." He also explained, "They use not only this year's grapes, but we have base wines from up to six or more different vintages that have been held in reserve."

They watched and listened until Andre moved on to the tirage or the adding of sugar and yeast and then bottled in strong, dark bottles, stoppered with a crown cork. "The second fermentation will occur in the bottle. They then rest on the lees for at least 15 months for the non vintage, and, for the vintage, for a number of years. They are riddled, that is turned and shaken to move the deposit to the neck. We use racks, the bottles staked forty to four hundred dozen high. The orientation is changed around the clock. The process can be done in three days compared to six weeks in the old method of doing them by hand. The conventional way is that the neck of the bottle that contains the deposit is then plunged into a tray of freezing solution. The bottle is upended and opened, and the deposit flies out as a solid pellet of ice. The bottles are topped up with a mixture of wine and sugar syrup called a dosage, stoppered with a proper champagne cork, held on with a wire muzzle, and prepared for labeling."

Joan asked why the champagne bottles are so thick and why the wire to hold the cork. He explained that the second fermentation process, that gives one the fizz, is under pressure, and the wire helps hold the cork in place. The bottles are thick to prevent breaking. He went on to explain that there are different methods used. Many use tanks, not casks.

They moved through the buildings. Other vintners often stopped him and asked him to taste a blending they were doing. Sister was enthralled and tasted right along with Andre. Even Mac and Arthur did, when Sister suggested they do so when a particular blend caught her attention. Joan took notes but did not taste. Elmore did not either.

Finally, he took them to his office and said he would like to open a bottle of his blanc de blanc for Sister. She insisted that was too much; it wasn't necessary. Andre patted her hand and told her that he rarely had as intelligent and charming a guest. He nodded at the others and patted Joan and said, "Your charm makes your lack of expertise unnoticeable."

She leaned over and kissed him on the cheek. "May I ask you two more simple questions? You won't be mad?"

He nodded as he reached for the chilled bottle and showed it to them all while he arranged six glasses. "Tell me, Andre," Joan asked, "Is there a special way to open a bottle of champagne?"

"Ah. A very good and smart question. First, observe, I break the foil. I keep a finger on the cork to keep it from flying away. Then, holding my finger on the cork, I unscrew the wire—six turns will do it. Hold the cork firmly: no need to take the wire off, and while you twist the cork in one direction, you hold the bottle at the bottom and twist it in the other direction. A Champagne cork should not make a loud *thwock*. You gently ease it out, so it makes just a light hissing sound: a sound like a contented woman's sigh." He raised his eyebrows at Joan.

"You hold the bottle around the base. Pour. Fill each glass with about two inches of champagne. Then go back and top them off. If there is champagne left, seal the bottle using a champagne stopper and place it back in the ice bucket. Do not top off the glass with fresh champagne after each sip. Frequent topping can mean the wine is never nicely chilled. Wait till only one sip is left, then top.

"You see there is an indentation in the bottom of the bottle, called a punt. Once there were sharp ponte marks left over from the bottle making, so making the punt was to keep the bottle stable and from scratching the table.

"One more lesson, Joan. For champagne glasses, the flute and its cousin, the tulip, are the most eminently practical. When champagne is poured into either the flute or tulip glass, the CO_2 gas dissolved in the liquid rubs against microscopic points on the glass's seemingly smooth inside surface. The friction causes the gas to burst into bubbles. Bubbles in any liquid vary in size depending on the pressure of the surrounding liquid. By virtue of the increased pressure at the bases, the flute and tulip encourage long bedded lines of especially tiny bubbles. We here like the slightly wider tulip. It is better to appreciate the Champagne aroma."

Joan just stared and watched Andre pour. They all sipped and sighed. Joan said, "I have never tasted anything as good as this."

There was agreement all around and Andre beamed. Finally he said, "Joan, you said you had two questions?"

"Oh no, the second one is too silly."

"No, no my dear, you are not silly at all. Tell me."

Joan looked at Sister, Mac, Arthur, and Elmore. "You won't be too embarrassed?"

"Ask him, Joan." Sister said nodding at her.

"Can you, Andre, tell one chardonnay grape from another? I mean, yesterday, the special grapes you used to make the blanc de blanc; could you put them next to these and tell which was which?"

He shrugged, and said with a touch of arrogance—almost disdain —and a slight toss of his head, "Of course." He quickly looked at Sister, "I do not mean to be disdaining. Sister, you could do this easily. I'm sorry, I wish we had grapes to demonstrate this, but when you get home in August, put your grapes against a neighbor's, and you will quickly see."

Sister smiled sweetly at him, "Thank you, that is indeed a great compliment."

"No, you have a very educated palate. All Masters do, but you especially."

The conversation moved on as they finished the champagne. They all thanked him. Mac and Arthur invited him to California. Sister said she would research the grape she was using and write him. Joan gave him another kiss on the cheek and a hug. Elmore shook his hand and said his kindness would not be forgotten.

Chapter 18

"Mr. Santoni, Elmore's on the line." Santoni's secretary said.

"Thank you. ... Good morning, Elmore. I assume everything is going well."

"Unbelievable. If I hadn't been here I never would have believed it." He told him everything that had happened.

Santoni laughed all the way through the tale. "I'd say those two are invincible. I would not want to be in their way."

"Joan played the head vintner like, what is it they say, a fine violin... or is it a fiddle? I know it sounds like a cliché, but, Sir, this one really fit. The vintner gave Sister the means to create the blanc de blanc. Then the second day, they went on to the making of other champagnes. The vintner treated Sister like his equal in every respect. Sister asked Arthur and Mac to taste those she found interesting. No one was left out, and Joan retreated to her role as secretary, until they got to the end. The vintner opened one of their prize blanc de blancs. Unheard of. It was the best thing I have ever tasted. He gave Joan a lesson on how to open a champagne bottle and the proper glasses to use. She rewarded him with a kiss."

"Are you saying, Sister's chardonnay is as good as their prize ones, those they use in the blancs ?"

"Yes, sir. Exactly. All discovered through Joan's cleverness."

"Then what have you left, today and tomorrow?"

"They will visit the Salon house and Taittinger. Mac and Arthur are spending time in the fields, bottling and learning about the casks they use there. Sister will do some of this, but she wants to know how the making of the blancs at these two houses differ from at the Krugs'. All three of these houses are renowned for their blanc de blancs. I suppose you could call it 'no stone left unturned.'"

"Are you enjoying yourself, Elmore?"

"Yes, I am. I'm going to spend more time with Mac and Arthur as they inspect the fields, and see how they choose casks. Sister is fascinating to watch and listen to. I don't believe there is anyone who knows more about the whole business. When she is confronted with a new area, she digs and digs until it is hers. She's so well grounded, it is a joy to watch her. Joan listens and learns and when she thinks Sister may have a question she isn't asking, Joan asks it. God, it's a wonder to watch those two."

"Sister is not a telepath. How are they communicating?"

"I think Joan listens to the conversation and tunes into Sister at the same time. I'm just guessing here, but I bet when there's a hitch in Sister listening, Joan then tunes into her more carefully, and asks a question. It makes Sister look very astute, when she interrupts Joan's questions and acts like she is trying to clarify it for Joan."

"When it was her question all along?"

"Yes, I think so. There is no way I can be sure, I don't dare ask without violating their privacy. It would tell them I'm watching them closely." Elmore paused. "No, I won't mess with that."

"Elmore, I wouldn't worry about it. I bet Sister knows very well that you know what they're doing, and probably Joan knows as well. They told us as much when they were here. If these French and vintners weren't so secretive, Sister wouldn't need recourse to Joan. So you have one more day there, then you leave tomorrow afternoon for Paris."

"Yes. The ladies will have two whole days to shop, and I have suggestions for the evenings for them. Arthur and Mac have some things they want me to look at with them. You know, I think it will be fun. Romano will be in early Sunday morning. We'll meet him at the airport. I'll catch an early flight back to England. He'll fly them on to Portugal. Is everything good there? Have you heard more from Galeano?"

"I told him you all were in France and why. That Romano would be coming to take our friends on to Portugal. After we talked a while, he suggested that I have Romano call Miguel since they went to school together. He will tell his second in command Mateo to have Miguel fully brief Romano when he calls."

"Does he suspect something is going on?"

"No. Well, I don't think he knows what is going on with his son. He said Diego's paying attention to business. He has the use of the company planes for short hops around the country on company business. Mateo has arranged for the men who manage the planes to keep careful track of where and when Diego flies. His father hopes if he does get worse they will be on top of him. He said he seems to be calming down. Even went home and got along with his brothers and sisters."

"I know both Mateo and Miguel. If they are watching him they'll be careful. Lets see what Miguel tells Romano. I'd best be off to the wineries."

"Good. I'll keep you abreast of the Spain situation." Santoni hung up.

After two busy days they left after lunch for the drive to Paris. The countryside was lovely, even if it was winter. He told Sister and Joan he'd gotten them a one bedroom suite with two large king beds. He told Mac and Arthur he got a two bedroom suite for the three of them. Was that gong to be okay with all of them? Arthur said fine: Mary told him he doesn't snore.

He handed Joan and Sister the list of plays and concerts, asking if they had preferences.

It ended with everyone saying tonight they would dine well and call it a night. Then, in the morning, Sister and Joan would be off to the stores, one fashion show, and just whatever. They all agreed to one play and one concert. They all had great taste so there was no squabbling. They all had been in Paris before, so sightseeing was not on the lists. He told them Romano would land early Monday morning, so it would be up early for everyone.

After everyone had settled in, Elmore lounged in the living room, having a glass of wine. His cell phone was at his ear, as Romano had just called. They talked business and travel times. Finally Elmore asked, "What do you hear from Miguel?"

"Diego is a slippery one. Miguel said he gives his itinerary to the secretary, then he changes it up as he goes. No major changes, and he always has a reason for the change. The staff just added it up to his general absentmindedness since the death of his brother. The only reason they know of some of these changes is when someone is looking for him and he isn't where he said he would be."

"Tell me, do they have more than one plane? And does he always use the same plane?"

"They have several planes. Not only for the syndicate business but for the wine business. They vary in size from simple four-passenger to two good-sized jets like ours. Yes, they are capable of flying to the states. Pablo flew one there, as did his father. He flies all of them. Changes from one to another almost every time he goes up. I asked Miguel if he has always done this. He said he doesn't know but will find out for me."

"Damn, this is sounding strange, unless it's a past behavioral pattern for him."

"Yes, I know."

"Romano, tell him or ask him to place trackers on the planes. Use ones with more power for the big planes. If he has trouble getting these, send them to him. Tell him we want to know the second Diego leaves the country. You and he can, of course, tell Mateo. Get a small monitor alerter that he can keep on him. He can keep the base elsewhere." he paused. "Report all this to Santoni. Ask him if he wants to tell the father. It sure would make it easier on everyone if he knew and approved what we want to do"

"I'll do it. I'll be landing at five a.m. Monday. We want to be in Porto by eight, and then check into the place we will be staying. We are expected at Cockburn around ten. It's a tight schedule. I can only hope it goes as well as it did for you. Elmore, does Mac have the proper grapes for Port?"

"I don't know. I'll ask him at dinner tonight. I know this is more his and Arthur's baby, but Sister will do whatever she can to help them."

The food was wonderful. Sister and Joan were beaming. They told the men they were looking forward to a great day of shopping tomorrow. Over the dessert, Elmore asked them what their action plan was to be in Porto. "I mean, what are you all going to look at, or for, to create the best port you can?" They remained silent and looked at each other than at Mac.

Finally Mac said, "I'm not sure. The steps that go into this are simple compared to the champagnes. What I don't know is what kind of grapes they use. Can others be used? If so, what? Is the kind of grape used the most important or is it the soil they grow in or both? The side of the mountain, the temperature, the sun, the rainfall, all of it. I guess I'm saying, it is all really important. Not just the grapes, but how and where they grow." He stopped and looked at Arthur.

Arthur smiled, "I've read everything Mac gave me and visited the growers and makers of Port in California. I've tasted their product. Some are quite good, but we both agree they lack something. Maybe it is the overall terroir—you know the soil, sun, temperature, rain; not just the kind of grape. Mary would call it the gestalt they grow up in."

"Are you asking, Arthur, can that be duplicated in California at Bodega? Or Twisted Hills?" Joan asked.

"Yes, precisely, Joan. We will look at the growing gestalt and see if we can match it to anything at Bodega or Twisted hills. You know, like Sister did with the chardonnay grapes. She put them into an environment similar to where they came from."

"Arthur, that's not quite right. We did just the reverse. Cat and I knew where we wanted to plant them, then we looked for grapes that grew in a place that was like that. However," she put her hand up to stop him, "We lucked out. But you have the right idea. Let me say one more thing. Mac, we know our grapes. How each tastes. If we find the right, what is it, you call it 'gestalt,' we can pick and choose before we even get started."

"Now you have me confused. Take the cabernets. Have you studied if some you grow in one place taste better or different, as a wine, than others?"

"Yes," Mac said. "Of course. But, then, even those change from year to year. We keep a record of all our grapes at both vineyards. You have heard the vintners here say how one season is excellent and another will only be average. We will not worry about that variance if we can just get an idea of what goes into the creation of a good port wine, from the grape standpoint."

Elmore sat and thought, "Joan, does this sound to you like what happened with the blanc de blancs?"

Joan looked at him carefully, and you could just see the wheels turning. "A comparison and tasting sort of thing. Hum, but in reverse. Like, we give you a selection of wines, and you match them to a port base wine that hasn't been doctored. A game, a challenge sort of thing. Hum, but will they play? And if they do, will you learn anything?"

"Can we blatantly ask them for that kind of help, Mac?" Arthur asked.

"We can ask. What their response will be is another thing." He shrugged his shoulders.

"Sister, do you know what your base wines taste like?" Elmore asked

"Yes, for the most part." She paused and thought about where Elmore was going. "You're looking for a shortcut aren't you? Well, not exactly a short cut, but if one of our wines was similar, and we knew where in the vineyard it came from, hum, it would narrow things down."

"Sister, thats a lot of ifs," Arthur said.

"Yes, it is. We do keep track of where our grapes are harvested from and what they taste like. Especially our reserves. That bottle and year are clearly marked by location in the vineyards—I mean in large blocks when they are picked. We don't just toss them all together."

"Mac, you brought nothing but reserves with us, didn't you? According to Sister you know where they came from."

Mac nodded in agreement, looking at them all, then looked out a window. "I'm not sure. I don't dream we can duplicate what Joan and Sister accomplished with the blancs. Arthur, will be going over the fields with me, and other parts of the operation, while Sister concentrates on the mixing and tasting. Joan will go with Sister as before. She will ask her usual naïve questions and work her magic. You know, we may learn something. You, Joan, will offer one of our wines for tasting, or whatever you did with the blancs. Hum, nothing to lose."

Elmore held his glass up for a toast. "I'm going to be sorry to miss this, but when I tell Romano what you may be up to, he will be delighted, and may be helpful."

Chapter 19

Everyone arrived at the plane at 5 am. It took a bit to get all the ladies' packages on board. Romano rolled his eyes, and Joan gave him a soft slap, "Be careful, child, or you won't get your present."

Sister looked at them both, smiled at Romano and put her arm around him. "She's just teasing, dear. She spent hours looking for just the right thing for you."

"Arthur, you're licensed to fly a plane like this, so will you fly second seat with me?"

"I'd be honored, Romano."

"Mac, Sister, Joan, I left some material on Cockburn, the first place we'll stop. If you'll peruse it, you'll have a step up. It's material a local company officer put together for me. Elmore told me about your conversation, I put some questions to him along those lines. I think you'll find it very informative."

"Excuse me, Romano, are you saying they'll tell us anything we want to know?" Sister asked.

"Yes, one could say that, if you ask the right questions. You're not a threat to them in the commercial field here, and they're close to Santoni."

After they were cleared to depart to Porto, and Romano filled Arthur in on the instruments, he said, "I'm concerned about what may be happening in Spain. I spoke with Miguel yesterday. He's keeping close watch on Diego and is putting trackers on all the planes he uses." He then went on to discuss Diego's strange behavior.

"Romano, do you really believe he means to fly to America and hunt down those he thinks may've had a part in his brothers death?"

"Arthur, I don't know the man. Mateo knows him, but only concerning business. Miguel, not at all; that's why he was chosen to keep an eye him, so he won't get suspicious. Diego likes to club and drink, just like his brother."

Arthur mulled over what he had been told. Finally he asked, "What does Santoni think?"

"He wants to call Jeffery and at least bring him up to date. He asked me to talk with you first."

"Oh, boy. When it comes to Mary, Jeffery has a very short fuse. If he rushes down there and hovers around her, she will kill us all. How is your phone on this plane?"

"We have a portable satellite phone." He reached under the seat, then stopped. "You know it will be the middle of the night there?"

"Damn, I forgot. I'll call her on the way to the vineyard. She's an early riser. Should be up by 5."

"Good. The ladies will want to talk with her, too. Take her mind off the message. I'll tell Santoni what you decide after you call her."

Palm Valley
Five a.m.

The phone rang, and, as usual, Mary checked the caller ID before answering. Not recognizing the number, she waited to see what, if anything, came over the line. She hated robocalls, as did everyone she knew. But… "My Lord," she said, "Now? At five a.m.?" She heard Arthur say, "It's okay to pick up. It's just me."

"Arthur, you do know what time it is here?"

"Yes, dear, I waited till I knew you had the first cup of hot coffee set up. I forgot and almost called you five hours ago."

"Are you okay? Is everyone all right?"

"Yes, we're fine. I'll let you talk with them in a minute. I also have you on speaker phone." He then brought her up to date on what they knew about Diego's behavior in Spain.

"Do you all really think he'll be dumb enough to fly to Florida, or even California, looking for someone to blame?"

"There's a possibility. Romano's contacts in Spain are watching him and they think he's acting very strangely."

"Arthur, if they have his planes monitored, that'll give us enough time to be on the alert for him." She paused. "God, I hate this. You know, at this hour of the morning, I almost think we should encourage him and then shoot him."

"You know your friends are listening and waiting to talk with you."

"Bet they'll agree. Okay everyone speak up."

"You got your gun handy, girl?" Joan asked.

"Yes, all of them. How's the trip? Are you becoming an expert?"

"You'll have to ask my boss."

"Hi, Mary," said Sister. "Yes, Joan has been more than valuable. We'll explain everything when we get home. Oh, and did we buy stuff…" They all talked for a few more minutes. Then Mary spoke briefly to Mac and Romano.

"Mary," said Arthur, "Santoni wanted to call Jeffery and bring him up to date. I'm afraid if he does, Jeffery will be camping on your doorstep and you'll not be pleased."

"Isn't he at the vineyards learning how to trim the vines?"

"Yes, but he'll be there tonight if Santoni calls him."

"Yes, and if that bastard Diego flies out and Jeffery doesn't know, we'll all be sorry. Maybe I'll just fly to Barbados and hide on the beach. Hell of a lot warmer than it is here."

"Good! Why don't you tell Jeffery and have him join you?"

"Don't tempt me, Arthur. I can't leave now anyhow. That Nocatee thing is coming on fast and furious. Thousands of acres and houses almost on top of us. No one is happy. No one is listening to what it is or isn't. They think they can keep it in trees forever. Oh, Sister you still there?"

"Mary, I am."

"Good, Sister. Can you stop by here on the way home. I have two horses I'd love to own. I'd never buy anything like this without asking you to see them. These are also dressage trained. They're really pretty, and kinda unusual. They are Friesian. They have long, long manes, long tails, and feathered, long, silky hair on their lower legs covering their hooves. They are very black, black and are youngish; about 4 years old."

Mary paused for a breath, and heard Sister laugh out loud. "Well, what do you think?"

"Mary, Friesians are lovely horses, and gentle. They generally have a high step and are elegant, I'd heard some were being dressage trained."

"Oh, you have described these two perfectly. I've put a hold on them till you see them. I know the people who have them. They are registered and have been shown but these people don't want just anyone to have their babies. They said I could ride them, but I wanted to wait till you saw them. I don't want to get too attached."

"Yes, I'll ask Arthur to fly there first. You sound so excited, I can hardly wait to see them."

"Mary," Romano said, "Did I hear you right? Did you say they were Friesian and dressage trained?"

"Yes."

"Well, I can tell you now: If you don't buy them, Elmore and I will."

"Ha," Joan said. "Can't you just see those dandies, all decked out in black riding britches and boots, coats, hats, and gloves, set off with white shirts. Hum, hum, they will win every medal just on looks alone."

"No, Joan, I think you're just describing yourself and Sister."

"All right, enough! Mary, we'll fly to you when we finish here. If you want the horses you know you can buy them. I may buy them for your for your birthday. Now, do you want Santoni to call Jeffery? We're going into the winery now. Romano will tell Santoni to have Jeffery call you before he rushes to Florida?"

"Yes, that'll be fine. You guys go work, I'll do the same."

Mary smiled. She thought, 'I'm so glad to hear from them. Not about this crazy young man from Spain, but just talking with them cheers me. Of course Arthur will want to buy me the horses.' She smiled again, thinking about Arthur. What a wonderful man! She was so happy he was running about in Europe, trying to figure out how to make Mac's Port and Sisters Champagne. She knew he would insist on naming them after both of them.

She thought about how much Sister wanted to make a Champagne out of her and Babs's grapes, like a final tribute to Babs. For Mac, maybe something similar but more for a final note for his family as the last of the Bodegas. Their wines were well known and respected. But a Port given birth from his soil and work. Yes, a true child from his soil and labor and heritage.

She and Arthur would do everything they could to aid in this unspoken desire of these two people they had come to love and cherish.

London
Nine a.m.

"Mr. Santoni, Romano is on line one."

"Thank you. Romano, I didn't expect to hear from you this early. Elmore isn't back yet."

"He should be coming in the door any minute. I talked with Arthur, and he called Mary. He didn't want Jeffery told till he talked with Mary. She reluctantly agreed. She knows no matter what is said he will be down there fast as he can. She suggested you call him and tell him everything he needs to know. As far as we know now, Diego is still in Spain, or at least his planes are.

"I've gotta go, but tell Elmore Mary has been offered two beautiful Friesian horses that are dressage trained. Only about 4 years old. I told her if she didn't buy them, Elmore and I would."

"As Mary would say, 'Oh, my God.'"

"I agree; I can't wait to see them. Good bye, sir."

The phone rang. "Yes?"

"Elmore is here. I'm sending him in, if it is okay."

"Yes, yes."

He rolled his chair back and looked at the door. Elmore, looking chipper and smiling, strode in. One look at Santoni. He slowed down and inquired tentatively, "Good morning, sir. Is everything okay?"

"I hope so, Elmore, I truly do. I have my senior staff learning about making exotic wine products... Arthur asking me to inform, and then calm, a volatile freelance crime fighter... Mary wanting to buy exotic horses... and now, Romano telling me if she doesn't he will. I mean, what could be better?"

Elmore thought, maybe I should go out and come again. "Sir, I got the wine part and Arthur, but I missed the horses, Mary, and Romano."

"Sit." Santoni thought a while. Then he couldn't help himself:

He had to smile inside and frankly admit that these additions to his family, or rather this addition of a whole new and large family, brought lightness, laughter, and, yes, joy to his life. He hadn't realized that his life lacked any of these till they walked in the door.

He walked to the window overlooking the Thames. He could see Elmore behind him in the reflection of the window. The wonderful thing about that reflection was, no one in the room could see it. He had used it over the years to monitor the room when his back was turned. Many times it had given him an indication of what others wanted him to do, or what they hoped he would not do. Life was not all that complicated, if you only used the senses that were available to you. Yes, he would love to have Joan's telepathic skills, but if you used what you had with skill and foresight you could do more than just get by.

"Mary has been offered the sale of two four-year-old Friesian horses which are dressage trained. She is having Sister fly into Florida to see them. If she approves, she will buy them." He watched Elmore carefully. Elmore's eyes lit up but he didn't move a muscle; just sat patiently waiting for Santoni to say more. Yes, he thought, that's why he is in charge of my whole business. He continued to watch Elmore as his eyes dimmed back to normal. If you were not watching you'd never notice.

"Romano told me if Mary didn't buy them he would, and he was sure you would as well."

He smiled as Elmore's eyes softened. "Well?"

"I assume they are midnight black, with very long tails, long manes and long hair on the lower legs. Probably registered as well. How lovely. I can understand Romano's remark."

"Yours?"

"Sir, I'd love them."

"Yes, I can just hear my rivals and the police, when they see you two dressed out in black as dark as the horses, saying, 'I told you they were devils from hell.'"

"As long as you don't show up in the box seat in a black tuxedo."

Chapter 20

Bodega Vineyard
Early morning Monday

Jack Foster was walking alongside Jeffery, watching him trim the vines. "That's very good, Jeffery. You have the hang of it—you're much faster now. Training the vine takes a bit more time to learn. At the rate you are going you'll be as fast as me."

Jeffery eyed him over his shoulder, "You're not just humoring me now, are you?"

"Not on your life. You're smart and you've taken the time to read the books Sister gave you. It just takes a bit of time to make it all come together. You know, when you have bright people to teach, it just goes faster. Like teaching Mary to grade the ripeness of the grapes last summer. Once she got it she just ripped along."

"Yeah, I can believe that she loves to garden. She grew up in Minnesota at Lake Minnetonka. Her family had gardens, and raised and sold flowers. She told me once it snowed on her birthday at the end of May. She was seventeen: Said she had to wait two years to figure a way to escape to Florida, but she did it. She has plants all over her house in winter, and the yard is filled with azaleas, camellias, and millions of trees." He paused. "Not much room for lawn... Excuse me the phone is vibrating. I didn't want it to ring and disturb the quiet out here... Hello."

"Jeffery, it's Elmore. Mr. Santoni wants to talk with you for a minute."

"Good morning, Jeffery. I hope I haven't disturbed you."

"No, sir, I'm in the vineyard learning how to trim the grape vines. How can I help you?"

"Arthur called to bring me up to date on Pablo's brother in Spain."

"His brother? What has his brother got to do with Arthur?"

Santoni explained the brother, Diego, and how he had been behaving, his plot for vengeance, and his searching all of Pablo's records and letters, and Diego's father calling Santoni and telling him what was going on. The son had been put under the watch of the father's men. Elmore and Romano know the father's men, and when they heard of the son's behavior, they had asked that the family planes be monitored.

"Diego seems to be getting better, or at least behaving more normally. However, Jeffery, Romano and the father's men don't trust Diego. Arthur wanted me to call you. He explained everything to Mary and she asked me to have you call her before you rush off to Florida."

"Jesus."

"She told Arthur she was going to go to Barbados and lie in the sun. He told her to take you with her."

"Sounds like her. Is this son, Diego, still in Spain?"

"As far as we know. I assume you're flying out today."

"Yes, I'll let you know when I get there. I hate to do this, but I'll call the local Sheriff in Florida and ask him to keep an eye out till I get in town. I truly hate to be unprepared. I think I'll call the Sheriff here as well and bring him up to date and ask him to keep an eye on Cesar Ruiz, the guy Pablo was doing business with here."

"Arthur said Mary is looking at some new horses to buy. You can go look at them as well."

"I knew those dressage lessons Sister was giving me would come in handy. Goodbye, sir."

"Trouble, Jeffery?" asked Jack Foster.

Jeffery gave him a quick rundown as they walked to the house. "I thought I'd call Sheriff Hall in Sonoma County, give him a quick rundown, and ask if he'll check on Ruiz to see if he has heard from this man, Diego, Pablo's brother. The Sheriff told Ruiz if he stepped out of line again he'd put him away for a long while. I believe Ruiz is on probation now.

"I can't believe he would have much to say to Pablo's brother. After all, Pablo cost him plenty. Since he found out they damed near shot Santoni, Ruiz doesn't want to get any closer to that man or his family. Ruiz may do some business with crooks, but he sure doesn't want the top dog after him. Let me make my calls and get on a plane to Florida."

"I'll run you to the airport when you're ready."

Afternoon in Florida

Mary pulled into the drive, stopping at the gate. The dogs were there greeting her before she had the gates open. "How do you know I'm here even before I get out of the car? Does one of you keep watch here, and the others at the house?"

She saw Sally's car in the yard as she drove to the house. She'd told her Jeffery might show up sometime tonight. She knew Sally would have leftovers set aside for him. He hadn't called yet. She knew he would wait till he had everything arranged; probably wait till he was on the plane, making it harder for her to talk him out of coming. "Hum, hum," she said, shaking her head. There was nothing she could do to stop him. She just hoped there was no need for him to be here.

Mary and Sally were having a glass of wine before Sally left for the day. Mary had told her what was going on with the brother of the man who was shot last year in California. She explained they were worried that he might be coming to Florida to get those who he believed were responsible for his brother's death. The phone rang. Looking at the caller ID, Mary answered. "So, Jeffery, when are you arriving?"

"Hi to you, too. Since I'm losing hours flying east it won't be till after midnight. Then I have to get a car at airport."

"Do you have your house keys?"

"Yes, I know how to let myself in. I hope the dogs won't wake up the world." Jeffery stopped. "They will let me in won't they?"

"After all the time you have spent with them, let's hope so. Sally has leftovers in the fridge for you. Don't worry about waking me up, just fix what you want, and we can talk in the morning."

"You're not mad, are you?"

"Would it change things?"

"No."

"Good, have a good flight."

Monday afternoon in Spain
At Cockburn winery

They all toured the winery, and after lunch, Mac and Arthur took off to the fields with the growers. Sister and Joan went with the vintner, who was in charge of crushing the grapes with vertical presses and determining when to put the grape spirit in the fermenting juice to stop the fermenting process.

The vintner explained, "The timing of spirit adding depended on how dry or sweet they wanted the port. Wait too long and you get dry sherry.

"The level of the grape sugar in the fermenting must declines from twelve or thirteen percent on the Baume scale to between six and eight percent, depending on how sweet you want the wine. The wine is then run into a vat, already about one-fifth full of grape spirit, whose alcoholic strength is seventy-seven percent. As the spirit is mixed with the wine, the yeast are killed and the fermentation is arrested. The juice, or must, becomes a young, sweet, fiery port with an alcohol content of nineteen to twenty percent by volume.

"The ruby is aged in bulk for two or three years. It is bottled young, while the wine retains a deep ruby color, and has a strong fiery personality. Young wines from more than one vintage are aged before being blended, filtered, and bottled."

He smiled, shrugged, lifted his hands in the air. "That's it."

"What is a Baume scale?" asked Joan.

Sister put her hand on Joan's arm, "It is a scale that measures the total dissolved compounds in grape juice, and therefore its approximate concentration of grape sugars. It is very useful in wine making since the number of degrees Baume indicates the potential alcohol in percentage by volume. The wine becomes a sweet, fiery port with an alcohol content of about nineteen or twenty percent by volume."

The vintner smiled. "Very good. I was told you were knowledgeable. It is good to have such people visiting here. Mostly we just get the tourist types. Would you like to taste a few wines? Some will be blends of several varieties but some are from our choice varieties. We did research into port grapes and identified our best varieties, which are now being planted in separate tracts rather than jumbled up together. We can taste both. Come I will show you, we will taste."

As they walked alone behind the vintner, Sister said to Joan, "What the hell, that's all there is to it? In a pigs eye."

"It seems so simple to get the wonderful Rubies you are known for. Surely you are keeping secrets from us." Joan put her arm through the vintner's.

"No, no, my dear, no secrets. Our grapes are from several varieties, as I told you. We blend them. One variety we have is the Touriga Francesa. It is widely grown, and one of the best. But it is not as concentrated as the Touriga Nacional, which is the most revered and the most suitable as a port. The vine is vigorous but produces less fruit. We are working with the cutting to be more productive and have higher sugar levels."

He looked at Joan, "Do you want me to go into the blending?"

"No, my dear, I am more interested in the tasting." She held on to his arm as they walked.

Neither could see Sister roll her eyes.

"What I really want to know is if any of our grapes would make a suitable Port. I mean could you taste our best Merlots and Cabernets and say if they could be a base wine for a port?"

"Hum, I don't know. No one has asked me something like that before." He turned to Sister. "In your fields, are your grape varieties separated? I mean, do you know which are more likely to produce a Reserve?"

Sister replied, "We have two large vineyards. Over the years, we have been keeping track of the areas the best product comes from. But, as you know it can vary some from year to year. I have brought a few bottles of our Reserve from both our Merlots and Cabernets."

Joan shook his arm. "You too know so much and talk in such technical ways, but I am a simple woman. Let me tell you what happen last week when we were in France looking into champagne. The vintner was telling us about his blanc de blanc. It was made from only one chardonnay. He liked it so well he set some aside for a plain chardonnay wine for only himself. I asked him if he would try ours and compare." She went on with the story. She ended by saying what neither the vintner nor Sister would have thought of asking, and discovered: "They found our chardonnay grape was just like theirs."

She shrugged her shoulders "I think sometimes you experts

know so much, you would never think of the simple. No?"

"Joan, this is very different. They have altered the wine with the spirits, changing the base juice too much to tell what it would taste like if not altered."

The vintner walked along in silence but obviously deep in thought. "Joan, do you know anything about making wine?"

"Not much. I came along for the trip and to take notes for Sister."

"I see." He turned to Sister. "She is like a blank canvas, so she can think a bit and paint any picture she imagines on it, yes?"

"That sums it up nicely."

"She has raised an interesting question. Excuse me Joan, but she probably doesn't even know it is interesting. She is in essence asking me if I can tease out the base wine in my memory before we stopped the fermentation and added the spirits. Then can that be compared to your wine?

"Joan, go and get your Merlots and Cabernets. Sister, you and I will sit and talk this through." He called one of his men over and sent Joan off with him.

Joan started to apologize for what seemed to be a frivolity, "No, no," he interrupted her. "Sometimes it is the purely innocent who open doors for us. You want to make Port. I know Port is made in America and in California, I can understand your desire to find an appropriate grape. You do not have our grapes but of what you have is one good enough? Is that the question, Sister?"

"Yes."

"I do not have a base wine to compare it to. So the question is: Can I tease out a base to match your wine? Or, should I say, find a wine that would make a good port?"

Sister just smiled. The vintner went to the casks and took samples from several different ones. He explained these were from different varieties. Finally he took some from a separate cask that was in a different section.

"Now, do we taste the port first, then the wine? Or the wine first?" He looked at Sister. "Perhaps the wine first. It has been less adulterated."

He looked up at Sister. She nodded tentatively. "We are seeking out the wine in the port?"

He laughed out loud. "You know, this is fun! I feel like a student in first-year chemistry."

Sister's eyes were sparkling as well. "I'm glad you don't think this all very silly."

"It may be, Sister, but at least you can get my opinion on if your best wines would make a good port. No one has ever asked us that."

"I can imagine it would be presumptuous at best. I mean, how can one ask that?'

"You can be a Joan, an innocent, and ask it. But, one vintner to another... well maybe not. No harm done, and maybe save time and effort for you, and fun for us to see if we can do it. Now tell me more about this blanc de blanc. Is it possible it is the same grape?"

When Joan came back she found them deep in conversation about grapes and growing conditions and on and on.

Chapter 21

Port Tasting

Arthur, Mac, Romano, and the head grower were walking through the winery toward the cask room, looking for Sister and Joan. They saw them in the distance and heard laughter, and even a giggle. They were sitting at a table surrounded by bottles, flasks, and glasses.

Joan sipped, and then sipped from a second glass. "Hum. I think I got it." She sipped again from each glass and, grinning, said, "Yes, this is it—or very close."

Joan looked at her. "Are you sure?"

"Yep." Joan was still grinning. "You try it."

Sister eyed her, "You know you're supposed to spit it out, and not swallow each sip."

Joan sat up straighter on the stool. "I am not drunk. I'm just happy." She looked at the Vintner, "I did not want to spit all your wonderful port out." She reached over and patted his arm. Turning back, she said, "Try it Sister! This is it."

Sister took a sip from one glass, held it a second or two, spat. Then, she took a sip from the other. She held that a bit longer. "Hum. Yes, that is close. Hum. Very, very close. Here." She handed both glasses to the Vintner. "You try." He took a bit longer.

Sister saw the men approaching, and waved them over to some stools nearby. "We'll be right with you. Wait."

"Yes, this is very, very close. Where is this cabernet planted?"

"It is on a hilly area, on the west-facing side, toward the sun. It is not an old wine, only a couple of years. But it was so good, we knew to label it a reserve."

The Vintner and Sister both poured more and carefully tasted again. Joan sat and grinned. "See? I told you we would find it." She nodded to herself and reached for the port.

Sister gently moved it out of her reach and held her hand, patted it, and smiled lovingly at her. "We'll take some with us."

The Vintner looked very carefully at the port they were tasting against. "This is from the variety I told you about. It is very special, the best of them all." He thought about it and turned to the head grower. "Charles, come over here. These tracts that this port is from." He pointed to the cask he had drawn the port from. "It's on west-facing hills isn't it?"

The grower thought a minute. "Yes, they all are. It was an area we picked to experiment with. You know we weren't sure, so we put a few of our prize grapes there, and a few down the valley a bit. The grape is so good it thrived in both locations. Why? Is something wrong with the port?"

"No, no, Charles. It is excellent, as always. Sister, can I ask your friend, the past owner of the vineyard, a few questions?"

"Of course. Mac, come." She introduced him, Arthur, and Romano, explaining who each man was, and then how the Vintner was conducting an experimental tasting with her. She told the Vintner the Bodega vineyard had been in Mac's family for generations, that he had sold it to Arthur and Mary, but was still their chief consultant and the one who wanted to make port. "He is the one who can best tell you just where this grape grows."

Mac looked at Sister, "You know as much as I do about where these grapes grow."

Sister smiled, "I know a lot, but not just where you gave birth to these particular babies. Are they planted together, or separated out, or mixed?"

Mac picked up the bottle and examined it, then smiled. "Arthur, this is from one of the areas we were talking about. It has many of the same characteristics as we see here." Turning, he said to Sister, "There is a large section that has all the same variety, or similar variety, but the others near it are equally as good. Maybe just off a bit, but both are delicious—as you know."

The Vintner reached for a second cabernet and handed it to Mac. "You mean this one?"

Mac took the bottle and examined it, "Yes, this is the one, Sister. Why do you two ask? Is something wrong?"

Joan stood up and hugged Mac. "No, my dear, we just found your port grapes." Mac just looked as the three sat there grinning at him.

The Vintner took his arm, and invited him and the others to sit and have a spot of Cabernet with him, while he told them a delightful story. Sister and Joan sat as well and beamed.

The Vintner told them what they had been doing and why; also who got them on that tract. He patted Joan's hand. After he finished, he said he would like each of them to taste a sip of the cabernet, spit, he grinned at Joan, then take a sip of the port. They were to see if they could find the cab in the port.

The grower looked skeptical but went along. He was not involved in the actual mixing and bottling of the port, but he knew his grapes and port. Sister watched Mac carefully. He spat, and then repeated the action. Everyone was very quiet. Arthur started to grin but didn't speak. Romano watched each of them and then grinned with Arthur.

"Hum," said Mac. "May I try the second bottle?"

The Vintner nodded and poured a bit in a clean glass for him. Mac, sipped, spat, sipped again. Looked off into space. Then, turning to the Vintner, he nodded. "You're right! This first one is perfect, and the second one is almost as good. This matches what we discovered in your vineyard. It puts a nail in it. Wonderful!" He looked at Sister and put an arm around Joan. "You two are unmatched. You have made a dream come true for me with the port and for Cat with the champagne. I can't wait to get home and try it all out. Okay, Arthur?"

Later in the evening over dinner. Sister told Arthur and Mac how lovely it was of them to give a case of the Cabernet to the grower and Vintner. She had given him a Chardonnay and a Merlot as well. They talked about the actual mixing of the spirit juice to stop the fermentation, and how much and how long to wait. Arthur, Sister, and Mac all felt they had a handle on it. The Vintner gave her actual measurements and timing. He'd explained the tasting and said it was not complicated.

Romano listened, and finally asked the question that was on all their minds. "Do you want to go to the other Port vineyards?"

"Would they be angry at you and Elmore if we don't?" asked Sister.

"No, it will just free them up for other things. They're just doing a favor for us. I don't think there is much you haven't seen. I don't know how you can match what you found here." His phone buzzed. He excused himself and walked away to answer it.

"Lets go back to the States. It has been a wonderful trip, and certainly productive. I agree with Romano: We have been very successful," Sister said.

Romano hung up and put his hand on Sister's shoulder and sat down.

"I'm afraid I have very troubling news. That was Mateo. It seems they have lost Diego. Miguel has been looking everywhere. All the planes are accounted for. Actually, he has been gone for two days. I fear they relied on the planes and trackers too much. Miguel is beside himself. He is covering all the airlines, ships, private air services. He's even tracking those in France and everywhere in Europe. He has all his men on it. Galeano has called Oliver, and they have everyone they can reach looking for any trace of him. Oliver called Jeffery first and he is using all the contacts he has in the US to find if he has entered the county."

Arthur asked. "Is Jeffery in Florida with Mary?"

"Yes, Arthur. I'm sorry I didn't mention that first. He had called the local Sheriff before he even got to Florida, so Mary has not been left without cover."

Arthur was looking at his watch. "Arthur, we can leave for Florida right now if you wish. You need not wait for your plane to get here."

As anxious as Arthur was, he shook his head, "No, no, Romano. I couldn't ask you to take your plane to Florida."

"It's not my plane, it's Oliver's. You know he will want me to get you to Florida as quickly as I can. It is pretty much a straight shot across the ocean."

"Yes, but you've had no sleep. Maybe we should go to bed and leave early in the morning."

"Arthur, you call Jeffery's cell and discuss the travel plans with him. Also make it clear we are all coming to Florida. I have horses to see." Sister had clearly taken charge.

"Excuse me Sister." Not to be one-upped, Joan said. "Tell him to get Sister and me a small suite at the Lodge, and Mac and Romano a room or suite—whichever is best for them. It's small, discreet, on the ocean with great service and food." Joan said. "Oh and a very large SUV."

Arthur was writing on a paper, jotting down time zones. Finally he said, "We don't have to get up at dawn. The time difference is about five hours. We do not want to arrive there at dawn: That wouldn't be good for any of us. We can leave later in the morning and be there before noon. That will work best with the Lodge and with Mary. Tuesday is a Commission day and Mary will be tied up all day. I'll call Jeffery and have him get the cars for us and the reservations. He can also tell Mary of our arrival. Romano will land at the St. Augustine airport. I'll assure her we're on our way home anyhow, and why. Finally, I want us and me not to worry excessively at the moment. The young man is operating without his father's network."

Romano's phone buzzed. He answered and talked a minute. "If no one objects, Miguel wants to come with us. It's the Don's request and Oliver's. He is the only one who would recognize him easily."

"Fine, make the arrangements." Arthur answered.

Florida
Tuesday, seven a.m.

Mary was having coffee, after feeding the dogs. It was a lovely morning: clear, a bit cold. The weatherman said it would be clear all week and stay in the fifties. She smiled. Her schedule today wasn't as bad as it had been: should be done by early afternoon. The dogs didn't bark when Jeffery came in. She had her door closed but heard him anyhow, rolled over, and went back to sleep.

He had picked up a car at the airport. She was glad he was so at home in Florida. He was used to coming and going as he pleased. She knew he was worried about Pablo's brother, what was his name? …ah! Diego. Well, if he was as crazy as his dead brother, I guess they had good reason. But, why wouldn't he go after that damn Hudson? He's the one who shot his brother. Wouldn't hurt my feelings, in fact I'd give him Hudson's address. Maybe I should put an envelope on my fence with Diego name on it and a note inside with Hudson's address and directions. She laughed out loud, putting her hand over her mouth.

"What's so funny at this hour of the morning?"

"Good morning, Jeffery. Coffee's in the kitchen." She then told him why she was laughing. "What do you think? Solve some problems."

"True, but if the Sheriff got your note after Diego killed Hudson, he might get you as an accessory."

"Hum, and wouldn't the developers love that. Now that you are here, what are you going to do?"

"I have already done a lot. I made reservations at the Lodge and rented cars."

"Wait, wait! What for?"

"Oh! I forgot. Arthur called me last night." He went on to tell her everything that was happening.

"Are they really finished over there? They didn't shorten the trip for me, I hope?"

"No, they're finished early, they were very successful and will tell you all about it later today. Romano is flying them over and bringing one of the Don's men with him." Mary stared to interrupt. Jeffery overrode her. "Diego has disappeared. The Don called Santoni and wanted his man Miguel to come and help find him, Mary. Not protect him, to find him and return him home, if possible. Santoni said the Don wants no more deaths because of his sons."

Mary looked out the window and thought, 'It's hard to think sympathetically about a crime lord's son.' Then she smiled to herself, 'Yet I am more than fond of Elmore and Romano, Santoni's men. What a strange world we live in.' She looked at Jeffery, 'How, Lord, is he handling this?'

"Have you arranged rooms for everyone?"

"Yes. Arthur, Mac and I will be here with you. Romano and Miguel will be at the Lodge. They were at University together. I understand Miguel has been the one watching Diego and feels very responsible for his escape—with, I might add, no reason to. He was given an impossible task. Sister and Joan will be at the Lodge, and God only knows where else. Sister mentioned some horses she had to see."

"Wonderful. I will clear my calendar for the rest of the week. I just love saying that, I hear that's the President's favorite saying.

Sally will be in all week. We'll tell her what is going on. Also, if you think this man will come here, we'll send Sally home. I want her protected. Now let me get off to work. Are you following me?"

"Yes. I have an early appointment with the Sheriff. Let me catch a quick shower. I'll be right behind you."

Chapter 22

"Well, Mr. Chairman, how did we get such a light day?" asked Commissioner Boat.

"Don't worry, Commissioner, it will pick up soon enough when Nocatee comes up. Be glad we get a day or two now. I have some things to do this afternoon. Lets see; we should be done before three," replied Point.

Commissioner Boat said, "Well I have a few things I'd like to talk about, since we seem to have time."

'Damn the man,' thought Mary, as she was about to reach for her light. Point saw her move out of the corner of his eye. She stopped her hand in motion and reached for a pen instead. 'Careful! If they think you want the time off someone will deliberately add on crap just to irritate you.'

"Did you want to add something Commissioner Paul?"

"What? Me? Oh, no. I just wanted my pen to make notes, Mr. Chairman."

His friend, Commissioner Ladder, came to his rescue. He knew Point had a lady friend he wanted to spend time with. "Commissioner Boat, I saw the time schedule and set up an appointment or two... unless what you have is an emergency."

"Well, no I wouldn't say that. I don't want to hold anyone's plans up, I..."

"Good," said Front. "My wife wants to go into Jacksonville and look at some new furniture. She looked at my book last night and penciled herself in. See?" He held up his book so everyone could see. "I told her that was fine unless an emergency came up. Is this an emergency, Commissioner?"

"No."

"Good. Let's go to the first item."

About 10:45 Mary looked up and saw a wonderful sight entering the back of the auditorium: two tall, stunning women, followed by five tall, handsome men. They were all grinning and waved at Mary. Mary's face was a picture of joy.

The Chairman, sitting next to her, noticed them looking at her. He leaned over, "Friends, Mary?"

She grinned at him. "You could say that, Commissioner. More like family, arriving unexpectedly. Could we take a five-minute break so I can see what is going on? Oh, and do come meet them." She reached over and patted his arm.

He looked at the clock, "I need a quick break, about five minutes." He got up and left the podium.

Mary quickly raced across the stage and up the aisle. She was enveloped in arms and hugs and kisses. "What in the world? How did you find me?"

"Jeffery did it. It's his fault," Romano quickly said.

Sister slapped his arm. "No, Mary, Joan and I wanted to see where you work. We just got in and Arthur said you were just down the road. We won't stay long just a drop-in."

"No, I want to sit up there. What's it like to rule the land? Can I try it?" Joan said.

"Sure. We have about 5 minutes."

"You girls go. We'll wait," Arthur said.

The three woman strode down the aisle and up onto the podium. "Oh, my, it does look great up here."

"Come on, Joan, you've stood at podiums in much larger places than this."

"Yes, but I have never had power over land, and people, and… you know." She waved her arms.

Commissioner Point walked up and pulled his chair out. "Please use mine."

Point was only about five foot five. Joan, at six foot, plus three-inch heels, towered over him, as did Sister. Joan smiled at him and sat. She spun around in the chair. "Oh, yes! I am now the Master of all I survey."

"Commissioner Point, this is Dr. Joan Bond and Master Sister Lopez. They have been examining vineyards in France and Portugal, learning how to make champagne and port. Sister is a Master Vintner, and Joan a ...'

"A master taster," said Sister.

Mary's eyebrows shot up. Commissioner Point smiled and said, "Those large handsome men are the lance carriers, I guess."

"Why, yes. How did you pick up on that so quickly?" Joan stood, thanked Point, and, taking Mary's arm, walked with her and Sister off the stage. "What a prick," she whispered to Mary, who broke into a huge laugh. "You got him tagged. Now what?"

"We go check into the Lodge and make dinner reservations for all of us—say about seven—and plan for tomorrow," Joan said.

"Good. Come to my house after four for drinks to see the house and your darlings, Sister."

Arthur hugged her again. "I'm glad you're safe. When will you be done?"

"At three o'clock at the latest."

"Jeffery will stay and ride back with you." Mary stared to speak, but he put a finger over her lips, shook his head and smiled. "Humor me."

When Mary sat back down, Commissioner Point leaned toward her. "A very handsome group. The women are magnificent."

"Aren't they?"

"Are they really all family?"

Mary turned in her chair. "Yes, in the finest sense of the word." She turned back and opened her book to read.

Sheriff's office
Eleven a.m.

"Hi, Jeffery. The Sheriff and Major Brown are in his office. We ordered an extra sandwich in case you hadn't lunch plans," said Martha, the Sheriff's secretary. He leaned over, gave her a peck on the cheek, and opened the Sheriff's door.

"Come in, Jeffery. Since everyone has arrived and are settled, will you have a sandwich with us?"

"Thank you. I left Mary hard at work. I'll pick her up at three."

"How many of you are here?"

Jeffery stretched out in a chair. "Well, let's see: your favorite, the tall, lovely redhead Joan, Arthur, Mac Bodega the recent owner of the vineyard Mary bought, and the Master Vintner, Sister, another six-foot beauty. Also a friend, Romano, and one of the Don's men."

"Really. My God, what are you importing into my lovely county?"

"Help, I hope. He is the only one who can recognize Diego on sight. His name is Miguel. He and Romano went to University together."

"Strange bedfellows, Jeffery. How long has it taken you to get used to them?" asked Major Brown.

Jeffery smiled. "Santoni, Elmore, and Romano are family. If you doubt that, ask Mary."

He paused and looked at the Sheriff. "As you may know, I spent Christmas with them. Two different worlds. They will not mix together, except through the association we all have with Mary."

"How does Mary feel about you telling us about them?"

"We didn't have any choice after the shooting last summer. Speaking of which, how is that bastard Hudson?"

"We have kept an eye on him," replied the Sheriff. "He cannot leave the country without checking in with us. We won't be able to enforce that much longer. Without cause, the hold on his passport will be lifted."

"I don't think he will be going anywhere without Santoni's permission. I don't know what Santoni will do with him. My best guess is he will not be returning from one of his trips abroad. The only reason he is still alive is he chose to shoot Pablo, not Santoni. He is a coward. He knew he would not get out of there alive."

"Now you have a crazy brother seeking revenger on someone, but who? You said Santoni told the Don everything. I suppose the Don told his son a sanitized version."

"Santoni said he did. The Don did not know that his son, Diego, hero worshipped his brother and would believe no ill of him. Since Diego's attitude and activities became known, the Don's had him watched. Miguel, one of his top men, had all the planes monitored. So the bastard cleverly got out of the country another way—at least we think he is out of the country. He has not hurt any one yet. The Don wants him home. That is why Miguel is with us. If Diego is here and we catch him, we will secure him, and put him in Romano's plane with Miguel guarding him."

"This Don of yours has been providing us, through back channels, with productive information on trafficking. Between he and Santoni, in just six months, we have closed down at least eight big operations. International ones that is. I wish we were doing as well with our locals."

Major Brown leaned back in his chair. "You know Jeffery, it is like we're working in two different worlds. What must it be like for you?"

Jeffery thought back to Christmas. "It has been an adjustment. Elmore and Romano were at the homes they and Santoni bought for Christmas. It was like a large extended family. We all exchanged gifts, went to church, ate together. Mary, Arthur, and the ladies all like them a lot. Yes, they know who they are. Santoni sent Mary, Arthur, Sister, and me a very special gift." He reached into his belt holster and handed the small gun across the desk to the Sheriff.

He and Brown examined it carefully. "It's beautifully made. Some kind of new material, isn't it? A new metal alloy?"

"No metal. Totally undetectable to any scanner. Also, the ladies can carry it and it can be hidden no matter what they wear. Maybe not a bikini."

"Undetectable. My God, I hope it's not going on the market." Sheriff Gray said.

"The young man, Romano, who developed the gun and material, is one of Santoni's men. He is here with us now. His father is a master inventor and Romano grew up playing in his laboratories. I think I can assure you it will not be on the market. In many ways these are very responsible people." He paused and looked away. "I find myself in a very gray world."

"Okay, now, honestly, what does Mary say or think about all this, or for that matter Arthur?"

"That surprised me the most. Last summer, when we first met them at the vineyards, Mary and Arthur treated them as they would any other wealthy buyer. Mary even invited the younger men to come ride her horses. Sister met them first to evaluate them to see if they were fit and able to ride the horses. Both men were dressage trained and so began the start of a relationship."

"Do you ride, Jeffery?"

He looked kind of shy. "I do now. I mean I have always been able to ride, but dressage, no. Sister has been working with me as a surprise for Mary. She has two new horses here she is going to buy, if Sister approves."

"Who is this Sister?" Major Brown asked.

Jeffery told them exactly who she was. He grinned, "I must say, she is the center of everyone's universe. Even Santoni loves her and trusts her with his private property—which gets me to the heart of the matter. If Diego is here in the states and looking for revenge, no one is going anywhere without protection.

"Mary is taking the week off." He then told them where everyone was staying.

"The Lodge?" asked the Major. "Whose idea was that?"

"I think Joan suggested it. It is small, very private and strangers will not go unnoticed. I believe she's as good as Sister." He went on to explain who was staying where. "Will you two come up this afternoon and meet everyone? I think it is important you know what the men look like, and Sister. Mary asked them to be there there at four for drinks. If you have time, call Arthur and come early; give you time to meet the other men. You may even be able to discuss some business."

"Business, hell! I want to meet this young man who created this gun," Sheriff Gray said.

Jeffery laughed. "I can understand that. I only ask you to keep its existence secret. Even Santoni was insistent it be kept secret. Romano's father laughed at him. Asked him who he was protecting."

"Who does the father create armaments for?"

"I believe the English government and law enforcement agencies. The material that is in this gun is a secret of the family, not shared even with Santoni." The Sheriff started to speak and Jeffery held his hand up. "Don't ask, there are relationships that are almost sacred not to be trod on. These kind of families prize them." He stopped talking and thought a moment. "I do believe they would destroy the formulas and plans rather than share what they don't want to share.

I don't think they hold most governments and government men in high esteem. However, they are English, and will help their country when and how they can by their own lights."

"I see you spent some time with Romano. Okay, I know your trust doesn't go out to people easily. I trust your judgement, but I will still try to learn what I can from him," he smiled.

"Good luck with that."

"Oh by the way, Jeffery, can it be equipped with a silencer?"

"No, it is only for protection in desperate places, and never to be used unless your life is in danger."

"How many were made?"

"You can ask Romano, I wouldn't. It would be considered rude."

Chapter 23

J oan, Sister, Romano, and Miguel arrived, with much barking and commotion.

Arthur walked out to the car to greet them, but the dogs were all over Sister, Joan, and Romano. Then they carefully sniffed Miguel. He stood very still and allowed the dogs all the time they needed. As Arthur approached they sat very still and watched him.

"Is it okay if I move now?" Miguel asked.

"Yes, they're fine. Just don't make any sudden moves toward Mary when she gets home. I'll fix snacks and drinks. Sister, walk about all you like. Joan's been here before and can play hostess for me."

The dogs walked the property with Sister and Joan. They ended up on the dock Sister said, "I can see why she loves it here. She told me she goes out at night and sits on the dock to be sure the Lord put the stars out properly. If it's cloudy she gives him a pass till next time. Then she says a prayer or two, talks to her Lord, uses the hot tub and goes to bed."

"Does she do this every night?" asked Joan.

"She said so, unless it is pouring rain. Then she stands under the overhang and just watches the rain for a bit. The dogs sit on the dock with her or stand outside with her. She said she is never alone but sometimes misses us terribly. You know Joan, she does the same thing at the vineyard at night. Either she walks the yard or goes to the barns or sits by the pool."

"Sister, I bet we all have our private end-of-the-day ritual."

Soon they were all seated in Mary's sitting/office cocktail room. It wasn't long before the dogs were off and barking again. Arthur walked out and saw the Sheriff carefully getting out of his car. "Call these brutes off, please, before I have to cite you for vicious pets." He hugged Arthur, smiled, hugged Joan and she him, then Joan hugged the Major.

He eyed Sister when he met her, held out his hand and held hers a minute. "I understand you are in charge of this crew."

Sister raised her eyebrows and nodded. Then she smiled at him and said, "And you, sir, are in charge of Mary's safety and health? A very precarious position to be put in, isn't it?"

"Praise the Lord, finally someone who understands." He put his arm around her waist, "Come, we can share stories."

They all settled in and chatted. The Sheriff finally turned to Romano. "Jeffery told me you are the inventor of his new sidearm."

Romano looked at Arthur, who rolled his eyes and tried to look away. "Oh, Sheriff, you mean this." Sister handed her gun to him. "Santoni gave these to Mary, Jeffery, and I. They were Christmas presents. After that terrible affair last fall he wants us to be safe when we travel. I can't imagine why Jeffery would tell you anything different. Romano is a magnificent equestrian, but an inventor...?" She shook her head, "You must have misunderstood. Why don't we wait till he and Mary arrive. I do believe he misspoke. Now, can you tell us what you're doing to stop that terrible trafficking in young women?"

Joan jumped into that conversation and off they went.

Jeffery and Mary were on the way home. Jeffery was driving. "I'm so glad you all are here, and I can't wait to show you and Sister the new horses. New, that is, if they pass her inspection. I called the farm where they are and we can see them later in the morning. Did you have a informative visit with the Sheriff?"

"Yes. I showed him my new gun."

"What new gun?'

"You know the one Santoni gave me for Christmas. He was fascinated with the material it was made of."

"Jeffery, my God! What else did you tell him?"

"What? What's the matter?"

"That is not for publication. It's a, what, what a family secret, and you felt you had to tell the Sheriff or anyone. What is the matter with you?" She stared across the car at him in horror and in anger. "Are you that angry at them or is it jealously? You haven't liked them from the start. They are, what, not your kind? They are something dirty to you, or what?"

"Now wait a minute. I like Romano just fine. I didn't mean to piss you off. I, I…" He paused. "I wasn't thinking. I meant no harm, Mary. I'm proud of the gun. Yes, I had trouble with the idea of crime syndicate men as friends. It went against everything I have worked against and fought against. I, I…" Again he was at a loss. "I'm sorry."

"You can explain that to Romano."

Mary turned her head and they rode in silence. Mary thought, 'God, his head is so messed up with this whole relationship, he can't even think straight. What can I say or do? I thought it was settling down. I'm glad Sister is here. Maybe she can help figure this out. After Christmas, I thought they were doing well. Even Sister joked with me about it. Said maybe Jeffery found a brother surrogate. Arthur and I were so pleased.' She stopped thinking and looked out the window, mulling over the surrogate word. 'My God is that it? Sibling rivalry?'

She looked over at him. His jaw was tight; teeth clenching tight. 'Oh, boy, if so, that's a tough one. I can't help with that. Jeffery is as much Sister's boy as mine. I guess it's a blessing that both Sister and Joan are here. Terrible time for this to raise its ugly head. I think it is best if I just sit here and say nothing. I'm still angry enough I can't even think of what the best words would be.'

Jeffery pulled up to the gates, Mary was out of the car in a flash. "Go ahead, drive up. I'll walk."

Arthur saw the dogs race out. He went to the window and saw the car, and then Jeffery getting out. 'Oh,' he thought, 'Where is Mary?' He walked out and in the distance saw Mary slowly walking up the drive. He looked at Jeffery, who held his head down and could hardly look at him. "Had words did you? Tell her about the gun?"

"What?"

"The Sheriff asked about the gun. Sister deterred him, but Romano is still clenching his teeth."

"God."

"Yes, indeed. You have some private explaining to do. Better take him out to the dock and grovel a lot." He turned and walked out to meet Mary.

He walked up and put his arm around Mary. "I assume, from the sight of Jeffery, he told you, and you took a large piece out of him."

"I did. It's times like this I'm glad I didn't have children."

"Do you believe he did it deliberately?"

"No. At first I did, but he's a man who doesn't make those kinds of mistakes. He just hasn't got his head screwed on right with these men. He's torn between liking them, admiring them, and hating what they are."

Arthur hugged her shoulders, and told her what happened, and Sister's and Joan's quick intervention and subject changer. "I told him to take Romano out to the dock and make amends."

"That will be punishing."

"Push his adjustment to reality a bit faster. He isn't much good with shades of gray. This may not be a bad thing. I can only hope Romano is more mature and adjusts more quickly."

"What about the Sheriff?" Mary asked.

"Joan and Sister have captured him and are telling them and the Major the stories about the wine country and Joan's tricks. Joan is also monitoring his thoughts, and will see trouble before we do. Thank God for paranormal friends."

Meanwhile, Jeffery and Romano were walking on the dock and Jeffery was doing his best to apologize, trying to explain the unexplainable till he was fumbling for words and repeating himself over and over. He was so pathetic that Romano's anger gradually eased. He just looked at Jeffery and shook his head. Realizing that Jeffery meant no harm at all, he was amazed to discover that Jeffery was overjoyed at such a wonderful gift, and at Romano's talent. He couldn't contain himself from showing it to a man he admired and trusted. Just like a kid.

He grinned to himself, "'kid,' huh? Romano, very dangerous kid, this one. I'm glad he is on our side most of the time." He put his arm on Jeffery's shoulder, "I've made some bad blunders myself, Jeffery. This will pass. But what about the Sheriff? What kind of questions will he ask?"

"I hope none. Mary took a large switch to me on the way home. I expect Sister will do the same. With luck, Mary will get to the Sheriff, and he will let it go. If not, tell him as much of the truth as you see fit. Like it's a pretty toy, not to be let out of family hands."

"You know, Jeffery, that's the truth. My dad and Santoni are very close. With something like this, they will want it guarded very closely."

Jeffery's phone buzzed. He looked at the ID. "Excuse me Romano, it's Sheriff in Santa Rosa."

"Good afternoon, Sheriff Hall, how can I help you? Everything okay at the vineyard?"

"Yes, Jeffery, fine. We got a call from Cesar Ruiz's wife. She came home to find him dead in his office. His throat had been slit. When we got there, his desk, chair, and the floor were a bloody mess. He bled out."

"My God! Let me walk up to the house. The Sheriff and the others are there. No sense repeating yourself. Hang on, I'll jog up." He put the phone on hold and ran, telling Romano as they went what he was just told.

He burst up the stairs and startled everyone by saying, "Sheriff Hall is on the phone from Santa Rosa. I'll put him on speaker. ...okay Sheriff, the whole crew is here."

"Good afternoon, Mary, Arthur, Sister, and whoever else is there. I just told Jeffery we got a call from Cesar Ruiz's wife. He was found in his office at home with his throat cut. We are still going over everything we can find. Whoever did this wiped everything clean, except for the abundance of blood. He didn't have any yard men today and the maid was out shopping with the wife. So far, none of the neighbors admit to seeing a strange man, woman, or car."

Sheriff Gray asked questions of Hall while they all talked on the speakerphone. Hall asked Sister questions, and Romano quietly looked at Miguel, who had paled at the news and quietly walked over to the windows and stared out. Romano joined him and put his hand on his shoulder. "Is he capable of this, Miguel?"

Miguel just shook his head. "I don't know, Romano. He had been acting very strangely. I don't think much of him. He's capable of damn near anything." They looked over at the Sheriff, and Jeffery motioned them over.

"Miguel," asked Arthur, "will you tell the Sheriffs your opinion of Diego and what he might do?"

Miguel looked at Romano, who nodded okay. He then told them about Diego and why he was in the states looking for him. He said Diego's father, the Don, sent him and wanted him to bring Diego home before he got into trouble. He stopped talking.

Sheriff Hall asked, "Is he capable of this kind of thing?"

"I don't know, Sheriff. I just told Romano I think he is capable of almost anything." He paused, "I don't much like the man, Sheriff. He is my boss's son, but I have never had much to do with him. He has always worked in other aspects of the business—I mean the wine business. You all must excuse me a moment. I need to call Mateo and tell him what might be going on. He will know what is best to tell the Don."

Arthur said, "Excuse me a moment, gentlemen. Romano, you need to call Santoni and tell him what may be going on. He will need to call the Don and encourage him to stay in Spain and not send any more men here. They will not be a help and may make matters worse. Tell him we don't know where Diego is. If he is here, we will get him and hold him till everyone figures out what is going on. Make sure he knows this is not a witch hunt. Also make sure he is well protected himself. Tell him to keep Elmore near."

When the Sheriff was off the phone with Hall, he looked at Mary, "Well, my dear, never a dull moment with you around."

She looked very sharply at him, then grinned. She put her hands in the air, "I didn't do it, Sheriff. I'm not saying it didn't need doing, but you can see we are all here. You might remember these men, the chiefs or Dons or whatever they are called, are your collaborators in another endeavor."

"Sheriff," Sister said, "Ruiz had many enemies. There will not be an abundance of tears spilled over his demise, except for his wife. I know Sheriff Hall is aware of this. If it got around that someone was in town looking for him, others could have seen this as a good opportunity to get rid of him. His usefulness may have been ending. Someone else may have seen this as an opportunity."

Everyone was ready to leave. The Sheriff asked Mary what her schedule was. She told him about the horses and the ranch. Said she, Sister and Joan would be out there for sure. No need for guards: They were all armed. She didn't know where the men would be.

They all left. Jeffery went with them, saying he would see them at the Lodge for dinner. Arthur sat down and had a fresh glass of wine with Mac and Mary. "Well, Mary,, it seems Jeffery and Romano got things right."

"I think they did. Romano was the more mature. He didn't have any baggage, and I think he cut right through Jeffery's. We'll see. This business with Ruiz is a bit scary. Do you think Diego did it?"

"Mary, I hate coincidences. Yet, I also heard what Sister said. She knows those people. So does Sheriff Hall. I think he will look at everything. He will first try to place Diego in the area. then move on from there. Anything is possible. It is hard to believe a young man without a record could cut a throat. Then, if he thought Ruiz had anything to do with his brother's death, anything is possible."

Mac nodded his head. "Ruiz has made enemies of his own. The Sheriff had trimmed his sails after his collusion in that attempt on Mary's life last summer with the cars. He was lucky he wasn't put away in jail for years. I know he has not been involved in the social scene since that time. Who would want to do business with him with the cops hanging about? Sheriff Hall has a number of people to chose from.

"Now, Mary, tell me about these horses you are going to have Sister look at tomorrow."

"Okay, if you two will tell me more about the wine and high jinks of Joan and Sister."

Chapter 24

London
Early evening

Santoni looked at Elmore. "I'm sorry time got away from me. Have I ruined any plans you had for the evening?"

"No, sir. I've put after-hours plans on hold, till this nasty business is over."

"That's not necessary, Elmore. You know I have bodyguards aplenty."

"Yes, but this business is very close to home, and Romano is over there. And..."

"That's enough. I understand." The emergency phone light blinked. Santoni picked up and as he heard Romano's voice, he switched on the microphone.

"Sir, I'm sorry to interrupt," said Romano. He then went on to tell them what happened to Ruiz: that the Santa Rosa Sheriff called them and the St. John's County Sheriff was at the house when the call came in. "Arthur wanted me to tell you to suggest that the Don stay in Spain, sir. They will take care to protect Diego if they find him." He stopped.

Santoni thought a moment. "Does Miguel think Diego did this?"

"He said he didn't know. He believes he's capable of it but doesn't know him well enough to say. Sister reminded the Sheriff that Ruiz was not well liked at all, and not to lose sight of the possibility that someone else might have used this as an opportunity to get rid of him."

"Hum, smart woman our Sister. I'll call the Don and tell him to sit tight. We still don't know where Diego is and more people won't help the situation. What are your general plans for the next twenty-four hours, and where will you be staying?"

"I'll be at the Lodge with Miguel, Sister, and Joan. Mac, Arthur, and Jeffery will be with Mary. Tomorrow, Mary, Joan, and Sister are going out to see the horses. I'll go with them to provide protection service. Jeffery will keep Miguel with him. Arthur and Mac will go where they please."

"Ha! Protection, indeed. If Mary doesn't want them and if Sister says they are good enough, bring them home for us," Elmore said.

"You know I will. Mary said they were beautiful."

"Okay children, enough. Let me get on to the Don."

Seven p.m. at the Lodge

Mary, Arthur, and Mac walked in. The desk told her their party was to the right, at a private dining area on the main floor. Mac looked around. "This is lovely, Mary. It doesn't seem too big. It's all laid out along the ocean, isn't it?"

"Yes. Paul Fletcher, a local developer and landowner, designed it. Back in the day, his family owned large stretches of land in Ponte Vedra. He sold, I don't know, four hundred or more acres of the thousands in that section to the PGA Tour for a hundred dollars. Then the big-time developers came in and bought the rest from him. He kept a large section now built as Marsh Landing. He had this patch left and built the Lodge on it."

They entered a lovely room and everyone found a place and immediately started to talk. Sister was sitting next to Jeffery and they were quietly talking, while Joan kept Romano and Miguel occupied. They started talking horses and Mary joined right in. She told them about the horses they were going to see tomorrow. Arthur and Mac asked questions ranging from cost to proper shipping methods should they purchase them.

"We can ride them tomorrow, I assume?" asked Sister.

"Yes, and you can do whatever is necessary to check on their health. The owners gave me the vet's name, and we are free to call him."

"If you buy them, Mary, the best way to get them to California will be by plane. The really good shippers will want clearance papers on them and insurance."

"Yes, the owners told me. Sister, it will be best if you go over all that with them."

"Can we all ride them tomorrow?" Romano asked, with a bit of yearning in his voice.

Sister smiled, "Do you have riding boots and breeches?"

He looked around and stopped at Jeffery. "Ah, if you brought yours, can I borrow them?"

Joan eyed them both and asked them to stand up.

"Oh, come on, just give me a size," grumbled Romano.

Everyone laughed, and he and Jeffery checked sizes. Perfect fit. Mary knew that, and winked at Sister. "Arthur you spoke to Santoni. Didn't he say Romano was on guard duty here?"

"Yes, he did."

"Hell," mocked Jeffery, "maybe he can shoot from a moving horse. Well, if it isn't moving too fast."

"And, my friend, can you?" asked Mary.

"No, but I bet your two beautiful guardians can, with one hand tied behind them." Joan and Sister stared at him and finally grinned.

Sister said, "Hurts to be bested, doesn't it Jeffery?"

"I bet," Joan quickly added. "Not only by a woman, but by two."

"Speaking of riding clothes do you and Sister have boots and pants?" Mary asked.

"Yes, we had a good time in Paris, bought new breeches for us both and for you. Then they had some wonderful boots... Well, you know a lady can never have enough shoes or boots. So we indulged ourselves in black on black. Didn't know the horses were black. We will all be lovely, won't we, Sister?"

Sister rolled her eyes. "Mary, we will give you yours before you leave tonight. They also had black helmets, so we got three. They are adjustable, so one will fit Romano."

The next morning, Joan called Mary and said they were on the way to her house. Mary said she'd meet them at the road. When they pulled up Joan slid over and let Mary drive. Mary held her boots up. "See how sharp I am? New boots, black turtleneck sweater and pants, too. Romano, I see Jeffery's stuff fits you well. We're all in black, I know that wasn't planned."

"I have always loved black on black," quipped Joan. "It does get cool here in February, I'm glad we're dressed for it."

It was a good thirty-minute drive south and west into the farm-lands of St. John's County. Mary turned off the road and drove down a long drive past fenced pastures interspersed with trees. To their left was a large house, and ahead was a large barn and corrals. They could see horses in some of the far pastures. Mary pulled up to a corral near the barn and stopped. "If you all would just wait here I'll get the owners." Mary walked into the barn. Soon two people walked out of the barn and joined Sister and the others at the corral fence. They introduced themselves as the Walterses, the owners of the spread.

"Mary will be right out. We just finished tacking the horses."

Romano said, "I'll go help her."

"That won't be necessary. Look, they're following her like chil-dren," Mrs. Walters said. "Mary told us she didn't want to ride them till you saw them and approved, Sister. Something about not want-ing to get too attached."

"Ha!" Mr. Walters said. "Yet she came out and would walk with them in the fields. They would follow her like children. Sister, is she a horse whisperer?"

Sister shook her head, "I have often wondered the same thing myself. They are beautiful creatures."

Mary walked them up to the fence. Sister climbed over the fence and walked around the near horse. Mary had moved the other a bit away. Sister talked under her breath to the horse while she felt its legs and examined it throughly. She then repeated the examination with the second horse.

"Mary, please mount up and walk, trot, and gallop each around the corral." She gave Mary a leg up. She held the reins of the second horse, then had Mary repeat the exercise with the second horse.

Sister nodded and waved her over. Mary dismounted as Sister mounted the first horse and rode it through the same paces Mary had, then began putting it through the dressage paces. She repeated this with the second horse. She then asked Joan and Romano to do the the same, but in tandem.

Sister, Mary, and the Walterses stood and watched. Soon, a car drove up and a man got out. The Walterses introduced him as the vet. He and Sister talked about the horses, and he handed Sister a folder of papers on both horses. He explained all that was needed to ship them was in there. He gave then the name of the company he used and explained it was the same outfit that shipped all the show and race horses from the better outfits in Florida.

He watched the horses work with Romano and Joan and, grinning turned to the Walterses, "Maybe you should up the price. I didn't know they could do that."

Mrs. Walters said, "We knew they were trained but I do believe it's the riders. I don't think we can put a price on them."

Just then two cars pulled up. Arthur, Jeffery, Miguel, and Mac got out. Arthur walked up to Mary, put his arm around her shoulders and said, "I assume we are taking them." Mary quietly nodded.

Mary introduced Arthur to the vet and the Walterses. Arthur asked Sister and Mary to join him to help with the final arrangements, leaving Mac, Miguel, and Jeffery hanging on the fence watching Joan and Romano.

Chapter 25

All the papers were signed, and arrangements made, for the Walterses to contact the shipper when Mary was ready. Arthur, Mary, and Sister walked over to the corral. Jeffery was on his phone looking serious. He put the phone away and said, "The Sheriff wants us to stop by his office on the way home. Since it's almost lunch, I told him we would pick up sandwiches on the way."

Jeffery turned and looked longingly at Romano and Joan. "Mary, will I get to ride them before they're shipped out?"

Mary put her arm around him. "Of course dear. If things go right you can fly home with them."

His eyebrows rose, and Sister smiled. "It would be soothing to them, Jeffery."

"What did the Sheriff want, Jeffery?" Mary asked.

"He'd been on the phone with Sheriff Hall in Santa Rosa, and wants us all to sit down and decide what to do next. Don't ask. He said he would tell us when we got there."

They all trooped into Sheriff Gray's office, arms filled with bags trailing wonderful odors behind them. The Sheriff and Major Brown were all ready at the conference table. Introductions were made to the Major, who looked at the ladies and smilingly said, "You are all just stunning." Then he grinned.

"What?" said the Sheriff. "Stunning?"

"Yes, indeed. Mary taught me that."

"Oh, boy. Let's get on with it. I thought it would be easier if we put Sheriff Hall from Santa Rosa on the phone and let him tell you his findings." His phone rang. "Sheriff, your call is ready," said his secretary.

The Sheriff switched the phone to speaker and explained to Hall who all was present. Everyone who knew Hall had to greet him.

"Okay, let me just tell you what I've learned. I spent time with his wife and showed her the picture of Diego. She remembered him being here with her husband. Ruiz told her he was taking him out to see the vineyards that his brother had been interested in. He said he would drop him off at the airport, then stop at his club for an early lunch with one of his buyers.

"It was late afternoon when the wife got home and discovered him dead. The vineyards he stopped at were yours, Mary. I drove out to both of them and talked to both the Salinases and Fosters. The Fosters remembered seeing Ruiz because he was there last summer. Nothing stood out. The men seemed pleasant and interested. Foster remembered hearing Ruiz telling the man he would drop him at the airport on his way to his club.

"I drove to Ruiz's club. The maitre d' said Ruiz had been there for lunch with another man. When I showed him Diego's picture he shook his head no. He had never seen him. He said the man and Ruiz seemed to be very busy going over some papers. He was in and out and didn't hear what they were saying. Only Ruiz was shaking his head off and on, and the man seemed to be trying to get Ruiz to do something. He appeared angry at times but Ruiz was smiling when they left."

"Sheriff Hall, did the maitre d' know the man, or had he ever seen him?" asked Mac.

"No, Mac, we asked him and the waiters. He was a stranger to all of them. The men in the parking lot said he drove off with Ruiz in the direction of the airport. My men got a description of him and went to the airport. They asked around and got nothing. When asked if he could have left earlier, they laughed and said, yes, several private planes had been in and out all day. We'll get a picture of Diego and have them go back out and show it around.

"We're still going through Ruiz's papers in his home and his office. His wife said we have to wait till his attorney comes to go through his safe at home and in his office."

"Yes, Sheriff Hall. Funny how the families of these crooks are as secretive as their spouses. We see that here."

"So you are going to continue searching for both these men?" Mac asked.

"Seems to me it could be either one of them. Ruiz did business with some questionable people."

"Sheriff, it's Jeffery here. You're saying Diego could have left yesterday, and the man who had lunch with Ruiz could have left your area almost that long ago. They could both be anywhere."

"Yes Jeffery. We're doing a forensic search of Ruiz's office and his home office. As careful as his wife may be, she is also frightened that some one else may be looking for stuff of her husband's. We'll go after the safes later today. But you know thieves, or business thieves, don't usually go around cutting throats.

"It is more the act of an angry person. Ruiz may have told this business man he had lunch with about Diego, thus giving him an idea for a cover-up of his own. We don't think this is a local break-and-enter robbery."

"Sheriff Hall, can you send us a description of this businessman, and if you find he came in on his own plane send us that as well? It seems Diego has his own plane as well. We're on the alert for that."

"Mary, when are you and Sister coming home?"

"Sheriff Hall, I fear for me it will be awhile. For Sister, sooner."

After they hung the phones up, Jeffery asked the Sheriff, "Do you still keep a close eye on that bastard Hudson? Do you ever just drop in on him?"

The Sheriff told him all they could do was drive by. He was not on probation, and they didn't want to be accused of harassment. Jeffery turned to Romano and asked if Santoni kept tabs on him. Romano shifted in his seat and said Jeffery would have to take that up with Santoni. Jeffery shook his head and mumbled to himself.

Arthur interrupted, "I'll talk with Santoni."

"I wish I could help you more," Sheriff Gray said.

Turning to Miguel, he said, "We have looked for your boss's son, Diego. But there is no evidence of him entering the country via private plane or any of the airlines. I do agree he's probably here somewhere, but..." He threw his hands in the air.

Casa Monica Hotel.

"This is very nice, Diego," Hudson said, looking around the private suite at the top of the hotel. "I appreciate your willingness to meet for lunch. I'm very sorry about the death of your brother, Pablo."

"Thank you, I was grateful to receive your call last summer when Pablo was killed. When you called, I knew you didn't kill him. Everyone did their best to tell me exactly what happened. They all said you did it. It made no sense to me—you and Pablo were friends. I watched you two when you were in Spain. I enjoyed your company, as did Pablo, and then you vacationed together. He called me several times to tell me how you were helping him find good vineyards."

Hudson was nodding his head. "Yes, yes, we had a great time. We were at that restaurant to celebrate our trip, even if we couldn't buy the vineyards. We had no idea those people and Santoni were coming there to eat. When Pablo saw them all together he knew he had been cheated out of the sale."

Diego looked at Hudson, nodded his head, "Why did he go into the private dining room after them?"

"He knew one of them had cheated him out of the sale. All he wanted to do was find out which one of them had done it. He was sure it was Santoni; not sure about that woman, Paul. Unless they did it together. But he knew it was a cover up. He actually thought Santoni had bought both vineyards and was lying to him, so his father, the Don, wouldn't find out. Santoni and your father were great friends."

"They still are. I checked the public records. They indicated that Paul owned both of them. Why would she sell—especially the one she just bought?"

"I don't know, Diego. Maybe she got over her head, or Santoni made an offer she couldn't refuse."

"I'm not so sure, Hudson. The records also show that Santoni bought a huge stretch of land to the west on the ocean, and across from it another large piece that is tied to two of his senior men."

Hudson laughed, "I'm not surprised! I bet the papers showed they signed everything after Pablo's death. In fact, the day after, I'll bet."

Diego stared at Hudson for a long time. Finally he looked away, got up, took the wine and refilled their glasses. He walked around the room, stood staring out the windows.

Hudson sat very still quietly, thinking, 'I hope he isn't as crazy as his brother. Why the hell is he even here in the States? I hope it's not to revenge himself on me. He knows I shot Pablo. Hum, at least he was told I did. He will kill me, I'm sure. Go slow, Hudson, he hasn't asked you what happened. He seems to have some doubts. Don't push it, let him come to this by himself. Just keep adding doubts a bit at a time. Let him ask, don't volunteer.'

Diego spun around from the window. "Hudson, you tell me. What really did happen in that room?"

Hudson thought back, 'Keep it close to the truth—only vary the end.'

"Pablo and I had finished dinner. I wanted to leave but Pablo insisted on going into the room. He told me he just wanted to congratulate Santoni on his purchase. But I was afraid there might be more than that. He had been furious all through dinner and when he saw them enter the restaurant, he got very quiet.

"Then he became almost jovial. He said he wanted to congratulate Santoni on his buy. I tried to insist we leave but he got up and said, "No, I'll just stop for a few minutes, to give them my greetings." Hudson paused and looked away. 'Drag it out,' he said to himself.

"We walked in and up to the table. He stopped behind the man called Arthur, Paul's lover, and spoke to Santoni, who was at the head of the table on his right. Santoni didn't even bother to introduced us to the other quests, about eight or more of them. He rudely asked Pablo what the hell he was doing there. He suggested he was sneaking around watching Santoni. Probably trying to steal the vineyards from him.

"Pablo got red in the face and said Santoni was the thief, not him. Santoni went to push his chair back and was reaching in his coat and Pablo yelled at me to stop him, that he had a gun. I quickly slapped Santoni's arm down and pulled my gun. Pablo grabbed this man Arthur and put his own gun on him. There was a lot of yelling, but your brother made it clear I was to hold Santoni and watch his men who were at the table.

"We were outnumbered. I could hardly keep an eye on all the men and Santoni. One of the men made a move, I turned to him and Santoni grabbed my gun hand, and, turning to Pablo, shot him."

Hudson was sweating and shaking and holding his head. 'God,' he thought, 'it could have happened that way.' Either way he still shot Pablo, only this way he had Santoni holding the gun and aiming at Pablo.

Diego looked down at Hudson holding his head and shaking. "Is that how your prints got on the gun? What about Santoni's?"

"I don't know. His men and the others rushed us. Grabbed the guns. I don't remember the rest. I passed out. Santoni's prints may not have been on the gun. His hand and fingers were over mine. Even if they had been somewhere on the gun, I'm sure they had a story for that.

"By the time I came to, I was cuffed to a chair. There were cops everywhere. They separated all of us and took me to a jail. They asked me why I shot Pablo. When I explained to them it was Santoni who did, they just laughed at me."

Hudson shook his head. "I finally gave up. I don't know why they all told the same story. Santoni is a powerful man."

Chapter 26

Wednesday afternoon

Hudson was sitting in the boat, actually hanging on for dear life as Diego raced down the Intracoastal waterway. Diego was standing behind the wheel, hair blowing, sun glasses on and ginning madly. He looked over at Hudson and smirked. "Not seasick, I hope?"

"No. I just haven't gone this fast on the Intracoastal. You got the fastest boat they had for rent. What is it; two 250 horsepower motors?"

"Yeah. The ocean going ones are faster. It's getting late in the day, and I want to see this Paul's home before the sun goes down. Does she live alone?"

"Yes. She has dogs and a day maid."

Diego raced past a place called Lulu's. Soon Hudson tapped his arm and pointed ahead. Diego brought it down off plane and Hudson pointed ahead to his left. "Up ahead is Barbara Jean's, her dock is the third one with the dock house on the end and the double decker top."

"How come she has two boats?"

"She says the Sea Ray is for leisure fishing on the Intracoastal and the other for the flats. I've been told she doesn't do as much fishing since she was elected to the County Commission."

"What is this Commission?"

"It's the local/county governing body. Law enforcement is separate."

"Are the police competent?"

Hudson looked over at Diego. "Why do you ask? Not planning to test them, are you?"

Diego had slowed the boat and stayed on the far west side of the Intracoastal. It wasn't more than two hundred to two hundred fifty feet wide. He slowly cruised down past the house, stopped, floated, and took out some binoculars. "Nice piece; heavily wooded. She's right up close to the water, but quite a distance from the road. Likes her privacy, I'll bet. I don't see any cars. Look, Hudson. Is that what you call a flats boat? That one up ahead that's floating along with the two men standing fishing?"

Hudson stood up and leaned on the windshield. "Yes." He looked at the water and noticed there was a good current flowing north. As he watch it, he saw it change and flow south. "Look Diego, the current flows north and then south. This must be the half way point from the the two inlets."

"What are you talking about, Hudson?"

"The Intracoastal flows into and out of the ocean in two places. One north, up at the jetties past the Navy station and the second is-south, at St. Augustine. It changes with the moon tides twice a day. It seems that Paul's is at the half way place."

"I see you just can't rely on floating in the same direction. If I'm floating south now, a little further it will turn and I'll be floating north."

"It doesn't matter unless you're fishing and want to cast into the current, or if you are just floating. You have to remember which way you want to go. You may have to stop floating and use the trolling motor."

"What's the tide drop here?"

"I don't know, we can get a chart when you take the boat back. I bet it's at least eight feet at the end of the docks. Why are you interested?"

Diego looked at Hudson, "Why? If I want to visit, I will need to know if there will be enough water to get in and out."

"You think you will be welcome? What do you do, when the dogs come running?'"

"Why, I'll have you at the gate calling to visit. I'm sure the dogs will race down to greet you."

"Me? She won't see me. She hates me!"

"We'll just have to find a good reason. Maybe with information she won't be able to resist. See Hudson, how close those boats are fishing near the docks? It's a regular happening. I bet the dogs even ignore them. See—I'll show you."

Diego drove further south turned toward shore and barely moving came north right near the docks. "With a rod, I'll look just like everyone else." He nodded to himself. "I need one of those flats boats and fishing gear. Hum... no problem at all. Dogs down at the gates, yes, it'll work fine."

"Look up ahead. What's that guy standing on?"

Diego looked. A was a man standing on what looked like a long surf board paddling with a long handled paddle. "That looks like fun. He even has a rod attached to the side and a couple of net bags. Thats interesting. Not fast but deadly silent. Gives me options."

They heard barking in the distance. Diego turned the boat west to the other side of the Intracoastal and stopped and drifted. He had the binoculars trained on the house. He could see three cars slowly coming down the drive. Three women and one man, dressed in black riding clothes, got out of the the first car. Three large shepherds were racing up with the cars. The dogs stopped at the feet of the shorter woman. She patted each one and they raced off to the next car.

"Brutes, aren't they?" said Hudson. "But they seem friendly enough."

"Didn't you notice Hudson? They all stopped, but at the shorter woman first, like they were getting permission to move on. I'll bet they're well trained. That's one reason she can live alone here. I wonder if there are others."

"Other what?"

"Other reasons. Do you know why she would pick a place like this?"

"She bought it in 1975 when she was still working at NYU. They say she spent half the year there and half here, till she retired. She's an avid environmentalist. They say when she retired she got involved in county affairs and finally ran for office."

"Can she be bought?"

Hudson laughed. "Unfortunately not. Those who tried never repeated the exercise and soon the word got out not to bother. It is even said she will play golf with a developer and then vote against his project at the next meeting."

"How do you know all this?"

"It's common gossip. Even gets into the press on occasion."

"Does she like being a Commissioner?"

"God, Diego, what do you care?"

"Hudson, you must always know your adversary. You are the only source of information I have." He paused. "None too good, but I'll make do."

'What an arrogant asshole,' thought Hudson. 'How the hell do I get out of this and away from him alive?'

He worried this all the way back to the Jacksonville Beach Marina. Finally he said to himself, 'Hell, Hudson, do just what you did with his brother. Go along for the ride and then direct the shot back at him. You won't be welcome back in Spain, but you hadn't planned to go back anyhow.' He rode along thinking 'maybe I can work this so he kills her first, then I'll shoot him. Save the day.' He chuckled.

"That was a lovely day, and interesting," Sister said. She, Joan, and Mary had just settled in the office/cocktail room overlooking the waterway. The men were walking around and out to the dock.

"Yes, I agree," echoed Joan. "But we still don't know where this man Diego is, or even if he did it?" Joan had sat down at Mary's desk. "Mary, can I use your computer?"

"Of course. I believe it's turned on."

Joan tapped the mouse and the screen sprang alive. "I thought I'd check my home email and a few other things. I love these Macs. Do you leave this turned on when you're not at home and working on it?"

"Yes, there is nothing secret on it. Just office mail and whatever I'm sent to read. I'm barely able to turn it on and off, and store a few things. I would not be termed computer literate. Oh, what I like the best is, it spells for me and I can look stuff up. Do you keep work product here?"

"Work product? I don't think so. If I'm interpreting you correctly, do you mean work I have created?"

"Yes."

"No. I read other people's work. May make notes for more info or something like that." Mary looked off toward the Intracoastal. She thought, 'that's funny. I don't put my thoughts or musing into print any more.'

Joan asked, "Is that because of your position as Commissioner?"

"Yes, I think it is. I have learned to be very careful I don't get accused of speaking out of school, so to speak. Politicians can't have too many opinions."

"Is this conversation secret?" asked Sister.

Mary and Joan quickly looked over at Sister. They both started to immediately apologize, then laughed.

"Sister, I'm sorry. It's my fault. Mary was so deep in thought and questioning herself that it just slipped out." She explained what the question was.

Sister smiled. "Mary, have you always been secretive? I ask because I wouldn't have guessed that, being with you at Bodega."

"No, I'm more open and just free-flowing there. Here, I'm closed up and careful most of the time. It's tiring I can tell you. When I get on the plane, I just drop it all. I shed it like a bad choking coat." She paused. "Oh my, I haven't put that into words before. Well, I'm glad covering my thoughts is automatic when I'm here. I'll tell you both something: I'll be glad when my term is over."

"Will you be content just messing around with grapes? I don't mean there isn't a lot to learn, but here the variety and activity is ongoing and forever."

"Joan, I didn't mean I would leave here and stop meddling around, but I can do that in spells, and I know where bodies are buried and where pressure points are. We have also put in some good countywide development rules to keep the worst away."

"What if bad changes are made to allow those rules to be overturned from the state level?"

"What a terrible thought! A certain kind of Republican, a lot of development money, laws changed, environmental regulations reduced... yes, the good we have done could all be washed away.

"Sad, but look out there. I'll still have my place, the waterway, and there will be others like me who will fight. I'll just join them and make the bad guys miserable. But right now I fear we have another problem lurking near." She shivered.

Joan looked at her. "You can feel something lurking near by?"

"No, no. Just the conversation and the possibility of what will lie in the future when the developers get their way."

"You think they will?"

"Oh yes, Sister. We're a very wealthy community. The ocean on one side..." She nodded and looked out the window. "...the Intracoastal on the other, and across the county, the St. Johns River. We are still quite rural in between, but that won't last forever. When the politicians start really chipping away on the land development laws, what we have now will disappear."

She stopped talking, and quietly mused about the future. "You know, the other day I was at a community meeting, and a new woman and her husband were there. She was complaining about driving down Palm Valley Road and seeing all the big trees being cut down. She said, why can't we stop that? Then she looked at me and asked, 'Why haven't you done that?'

"One of my friends and neighbors told her that the Commissioner was doing everything she could to slow it down. But when rich folks moved in and wanted the trees cut so they could put up 'McMansions,' it was hard to stop all of it."

Joan laughed, "I assume this lady had just put a 'McMansion' up."

"Yep, once her ten thousand square foot house went up, and the driveway and swimming pool and whatever, that didn't leave much room for big oaks."

Chapter 27

Wednesday evening

Everyone changed clothes and met at 'Ruth Crisp,' where Arthur had reservations. Mary called it a ritzy steak house, then proceeded to complained about the prices while perusing the menu. Joan said, if she didn't hush she would make her pay the whole bill. The boys said they would split the bill and Arthur told them to forget it. They could find a good place to eat in St. Augustine tomorrow and pay for that.

Sister listened to all this and smiled. She took Mary's hand. "Isn't it wonderful to have such a lovely big family that is always working in harmony? I did miss all of you when you left last summer."

Mary laughed, squeezed Sister's hand back. "I do, too, but I try not to think about it. There isn't much I can do about it. But I will be taking time off more frequently. I think the key is to not tell anyone ahead of time. I'm looking at the schedule of the planning department to see what's in the works. Then I'll plan around it. I also have some staff that like me a lot, who are well placed. If they try and slip something bad in, they will call me."

Mary was quiet for a minute, then grinned, "You know Sister, Arthur keeps telling me I have a private plane at my beck and call and I can go when I want, whereever I want, immediately." She laughed. "If they try and pull a fast one, I'll just walk in the door and take my seat. Surprise hell out of them."

Sister looked at her and laughed. "You know, I bet you will, and even hope they do."

"You know, Sister, they aren't bad people. They're like a lot of politicians: They think now that when they are elected, they can do whatever they want. If the rules say no, they just ignore them or write new ones."

"Don't the citizens get mad?"

"Yes, when and if they find out. If it's not in their back yard, they

175

may not find out or they don't care. There're just not enough environmentally caring people around. The man on the street calls them nuts and tree huggers. It will change as more people move into the county but that may be too late."

"So, what can you do?"

"Me, well I just keep harping on controlling growth, saving the trees, passing turtle ordinances, cleaning up the trashy signs, building more parks for kids—you know, stuff like that, all over. I figure if you like one of the things I do, I may not have to fight you so bad on the others."

"Does it work?" Sister asked.

"Hum. Let me put it this way: If a mother yells at her kids to pick up their clothes, wipe their shoes off when they come in, make the bed, clean the tub, etc., a lot of the time they do it just to shut her up. So I'm practicing mothering."

It had gotten quiet at the table. Mary looked up, surprised, when she heard them all laughing at her remarks. "Well, it works!"

Over dessertc they talked about what they would do tomorrow.

Romano, Jeffery, and Miguel said they wanted to go back to that ranch and ride the new horses. Arthur and Mac said they were going to the winery in St. Augustine, if any of the ladies wanted to come along.

Sister asked Mary if she was staying home and got a nod. She said, if Mary didn't mind, she would join her and sit in the window, watch the boats go by, and read a new book she had. Joan said after she dropped Sister off at Mary's, she would go look at the local shops.

Thursday morning

Joan dropped Sister off just as Sally was leaving. They introduced themselves. Sally told her she had come early to straighten up after the men, and now she had a dentist appointment. They stood and chatted a few minutes. Sister asked her if she was coming out to California this coming summer. Sally told her only if Sister would let her help with the canning and other work. Also, her husband would help with work.

They smiled at each other. Each had met the other's expectations of what Mary had described. The dogs leaped around Sister's feet and raced to the house to announce her. It didn't take long for the two of them to get into their old relationship. Sister in the big chair by the window, reading, and Mary behind her desk.

They exchanged the odd remark: Mary after a phone call, and Sister about a boat or two going by. Sister was about to draw Mary's attention to a boat with one man standing and fishing near the dock, when the dogs starting barking and making a lot of noise. They ran off toward the road and barked and barked, not stopping.

"What the hell?" Mary finally said, as she stood and walked to the windows facing the long drive toward the road. Sister joined her. "What's going on, Mary?"

"I can't see through the damn trees. It's not like them to carry on so long. I can't see a car, but then it's hard to see from here." They stood there and listened to the non-stopping barking.

"Oh hell, I'll walk down and see." Mary muttered.

"I'll go with you, stretch my legs. Time for a break." They both grabbed jackets and headed down the stairs. Sister came out the carport door with Mary behind her. A man stepped behind Mary and put a gun to her head and an arm around her neck.

"Stop right here. Either of you move, and I'll put a bullet through this one's head." He paused, then said, "I assume you're Dr. Paul," to Mary. Mary didn't answer right away. He jerked her head. "Are you?"

"Yes. Yes, I am. What do you want? I don't keep much money in the house."

Sister was eying him carefully, "I'm not sure it's money he wants, Mary."

He remained behind Mary. She couldn't see him. "Well, what do you want?"

He jerked her back as he stepped away from the door. "You—get in the house." He waved at Sister. "Go on, just step inside and away from the door." He followed her in, dragging Mary along.

"Now step over there. Good." He walked to the stairs with Mary, dragging her up the stairs behind him.

"Now, I want you to call the dogs," he said to Sister. "Hear?

They've stopped barking. When they get here you let them in and lock the door behind them. Then you come upstairs and shut that door as well. I want them locked up down here."

"Whatever for?" asked Mary. "They are very gentle creatures."

He jabbed the gun into her neck. "I'm not a fool, lady. Shut the hell up. You," he said to Sister, "Understand me?"

"Yes." Sister kept her head bowed in a subservient manner.

He got Mary up the stairs and into the living room. He called down to Sister, "When you have the dogs locked, come up here. Don't let them out. I'll kill them if you do. Understand?"

"Yes."

The man pulled a dining room chair out and slammed Mary down into it. He stood behind her with the gun at her head. Mary still hadn't had a good look at him. Her pulse had slowed a bit, but she still had no idea what was happening and why. "Who are you?" she finally asked.

"Just shut up. I'll ask the questions."

They heard the dogs barking as they raced to the house at Sister's call. They could hear Sister talking to them. Soon she knocked at the door and slowly turned the knob.

"Come in. Shut the door and throw the lock." He pulled Mary back toward the porch, while Sister shut the door and fiddled with the lock.

He looked around and told Sister to go and unlock the sliding doors to the porch. He grabbed hold of Mary again and forced her to walk in front of him through the house to be sure they were alone. He put them both in the office/cocktail area. He sat behind Mary's desk where he could see them, as well as the side porch and the living room.

Mary stared at him and then glanced over at Sister, who barely nodded her head.

"Nice place you have here, Dr. Paul. Great view."

"Thank you. Would you mind introducing yourself?"

"Diego Galeano." He was sitting in Mary's desk chair, he swept his hand out and around in front of himself, as if bowing.

"Yes, I can see the resemblance. I met your brother Pablo last summer when he visited my vineyard." She paused and looked Diego in the eyes. "One part of me is deeply sorry for you and your family's loss. But if his companion, Hudson, had not shot him, we wouldn't be here talking today."

Diego stared at her, then took a deep breath. "That, Dr. Paul, is not what I was told happened."

"Didn't Santoni tell your father the very next day what had happened?"

"Ah yes, Santoni: the ever faithful loyal friend. Of course he would tell my father that Hudson shot him. How could he admit to shooting my brother himself?"

"You think that Santoni shot your brother. Whyever would would he do such a thing? Shoot his best friend's son?" Mary threw her hands in the air, "I, I never, " she stuttered a bit shaking her head. "Where did you get such an outrageous idea?"

Mary looked at Sister, who continued to stare at Diego, never making a move. My God, thought Mary, is Sister in shock? No, Sister wouldn't shock easily. What the hell is wrong with her? She started to reach over and put her hand on Sister's arm, when Diego said in a loud voice "Don't move. Sit back in that chair, Dr. Paul."

Mary looked back at Diego then turned her head toward Sister, who never moved an inch.

"These blacks, no matter how light skinned, scare easily. They make good hands in the fields, to cook and do that kind of work, but in a pinch they are useless. Look at her. I'm surprised she hasn't fainted."

Mary glanced over at Sister again and deliberately shrugged her shoulders. "She only comes once a week to clean. I suppose that gun you're pointing at us scares her. Whereever did you get the idea that Santoni shot your brother? He never even had a gun. He didn't need to: His men were there."

They heard feet pounding up the outside stairs, Mary turned her head a bit and heard Diego say, "Why he," nodding his head toward the porch behind Mary, "told us." Hudson came into view, followed by the noise of the dogs' furious and seemingly endless barking from down stairs.

The phone had been ringing, and he had let it ring. Finally, it started again. Mary said, "I had better answer it, or someone will begin to wonder where I am."

"Why?" growled Diego.

"Because they know I'm working from home and I told them I would be available to them all day."

"Here, God damn it answer it!" He tossed her the phone as he pointed the gun at Sister. "One false word and she gets it first. Then shut those damn dogs up."

"Let me," Hudson said. "One shot is all it will take, then we can get out of here."

"Shut up Hudson. I'm not done here yet."

"Hello, hello," Mary said.

"Why are the dogs barking?" Joan asked.

"It's the maid. She got mad and locked them in the basement."

"Hum," said Joan. "Is that the new maid who isn't very good with the dogs?"

"Yes, I'm getting rid of her. I'm sending her down stairs to try and shut them up again. What do you want? You know this is my day to work at home."

"How many of them?" Joan asked.

"Yes, I told you do both of the packets and send them out today." Mary rolled her eyes at Diego.

"Get off the phone," he snarled.

"Goodbye, and don't call again today."

Chapter 28

Thursday
Late morning

Romano was sitting on the fence watching Miguel and Jeffery putting the two beautiful black Friesian horses through their paces. He was smiling to himself. Jeffery told him Sister was teaching him, as a surprise for Mary. He was also pleased that Jeffery could admit that he needed lessons, and by his apology about the gun.

He knew how hard it was for Jeffery to adjust to him and Elmore being friends with Mary's larger family, much less Santoni. Hell, he and Elmore had never had cops, or whatever Jeffery was, as friends either. He loved his time at school in England; he was just another student, like Elmore and Miguel. Here in America, with these people, he was also being treated as an equal, but when he and Miguel went back to their bosses to work it was another world.

He shook his head and told himself, 'Romano, be glad you have met such grand people. Now just concentrate on getting that bastard Diego back to Spain, alive.' He saw Jeffery stop riding and pull out his phone. He appeared to be listening, then he made a few remarks and, putting the phone away, rode over to Romano.

"That was Arthur. He asked us to meet him at the Sheriff's office now." He waved Miguel over and told him they needed to put the horses up and leave.

They did so rapidly, untacking them and giving them a quick rub, and some water and a cup of grain. Romano had gone up to the house and told the Walters they had been called away and had put the horses up.

On the way to the Sheriff's office, which was just a few miles away, Jeffery said, "Arthur told me the Sheriff had some news for us."

They all but ran into his office, the secretary having waved them on to the Sheriff. "Sit, gentlemen. Arthur is right behind you."

They had just settled when Arthur and Mac walked in. The Sheriff began by telling them that they had circulated pictures of Diego to all hotels and B&Bs. The manager of the Casa Monica had called them. One of his bar men told him when he saw the picture this morning that he had seen the man yesterday; that he was having lunch with another man. "I sent one of my men over with pictures of Hudson."

"I knew it," Jeffery said. "We should have sat on him right away."

The Sheriff raised his eyebrows, "Jeffery, we could not follow the man without reason." Jeffery started to speak. "No, Jeffery, we are not secret agents. We are local cops, and as such we must play within the rules until given reason not to."

Again Jeffery started to speak, but the Sheriff went on. "I think we have reason now. I have placed two cars near Hudson's house. I also sent two to cruise by Mary's. Can you think of anything else?"

"Have you called her?" Jeffery asked.

"Yes, but there was no answer."

"Try her cell phone." There was silence. Finally the Sheriff said, "There was no answer there either. I believe it wasn't turned on."

"Why?" Romano asked.

"Because she is a Luddite, that's why." Jeffery said, disgusted.

"That's enough, Jeffery," Arthur grumbled.

"But Arthur, she knows she in danger. How difficult can she be?"

"Excuse me," Miguel said. "What is a Luddite?"

"Miguel," Arthur replied. "Mary does not take well to new gadgets. She got a cell phone because the drive to and from St. Augustine at night could be dangerous, and she's a Commissioner. When she gets home she shuts it off. She says she has a phone at home, three big dogs, and a gun."

"But, Arthur, she got cell phones for a number of the employees at the vineyards," Mac said.

"Yes, she discussed it with the Fosters, the Salinases, and Sister. They all agreed it would save a lot of labor, time and money, but she doesn't carry one herself when she's there. She uses a computer," Mac said.

"Just barely."

"Thats enough, Jeffery. If it was up to you, she would be armed to the teeth and have a body guard with her all the time.'

The Sheriff chuckled, "Her past record would suggest that wouldn't be a bad idea."

Arthur threw his hands in the air, "You all are very brave and mouthy in her absence. The truth is if she were different she wouldn't be Mary. Also, as to what else can we do, would it be possible to have you send a boat up there to just hang around until we get home?"

"Yes, Major Brown is getting one of the boys' fishing boats outfitted and they will be on the way shortly. They can fish the docks near Mary and the banks across the waterway. Now, if you want to be on your way, I'll excuse you and we will talk later."

They were just coming up US1 ready to turn onto Palm Valley road. Arthur was in the car with Jeffery and Mac when Jeffery's phone rang. "Yes, Sheriff?"

"My men just drove by and there's a car parked on the roadside in front of Mary's house." He described the car.

"That's Joan's rental. Tell them to park nearby, but not to enter the property."

"You sure you don't want them to drive in?"

Jeffery looked at everyone in the car. "Sheriff, Joan would not leave the car on the road unless she suspects something is wrong. If they burst in they may get everyone killed. It may set the dogs off. If they are not barking, then someone has quieted them." He turned to Arthur and explained his reasoning. "Well, sir, do we wait and trust Joan and the rest?"

Arthur looked at Mac. "After spending a week with Sister and Joan—and now throw in Mary—I think waiting till we get there is best. I trust all three. If the dogs are not barking, either they have been shot or are being kept quiet by one of the women."

The Sheriff said. "I agree. I'll tell my men to follow your orders."

Jeffery thought as he floored the pedal and raced across Palm Valley road, 'Wait: Yes, Arthur is right. I hate trusting amateurs. He worked the problem silently in his head. Then he remembered Sister telling him very gently last winter to wait and trust his new friends and Mary.

Joan had seen the police cars driving past the house and slowing to look up the drive. She slowed, turned back and parked on the side of the road by the neighbors. She called and could hear the dogs barking in the distance.

When Mary answered, she asked her why the dogs were barking. She was told the maid got mad and locked them in the basement. Joan asked if that was the new maid who wasn't good with dogs . Mary said yes and told her she was getting rid of her, and now she was sending her downstairs to shut the dogs up. Joan thought, 'Oh oh.' When she asked how many, she was told something about two packets and not to call again, and the phone was hung up.

Joan quickly dialed Jeffery's number. She wasted no words when he answered. She quickly told him there seemed to be two extra people in the house, no cars in the drive. She was going up to the house through the trees because she thought Mary was sending Sister to the basement to shut the dogs up. She would try and get some information from Sister. She had her gun and they were not to storm the house and get Mary killed. She also told him to be silent; she would leave her phone open to him.

Jeffery covered his phone's mouthpiece and relayed Joan's message. "Call the Sheriff, Arthur. Tell him what Joan said. Also tell him it sounds like a hostage situation. We will approach up the sides through the trees. That damn house is almost all glass.

"Tell the police to be very discrete, to fish, not look at the house. Then call Romano and Miguel. Tell them to follow us and park behind us."

"How did they get in?" Mac asked.

"Probably from the waterway. They must have planned this out yesterday after they left the hotel. I don't know Diego, but Hudson is a sneak and a coward. He wouldn't hesitate to shoot anyone who was a threat to him and then lie, like he did last summer." He paused. "Miguel said he doesn't know Diego, except to say he was out of his mind over the death of his brother. Diego didn't seem to want to believe what Santoni told his father about what happened—that it was his brother who wanted to kill all of them."

"I guess we will have to hope he isn't as crazy as his brother," Arthur said. "Look; the bridge is just ahead, another few minutes. Jeffery, I'm not staying in the car. I want to leave Mac here to deal with the police. You approach up the north side with Romano. It is the least protected. You two are trained to move in a more stealthy manner. I'll come up the south side with Miguel, in case the dogs start up again. They won't bark at me or at you. We'll hide under the car port. I think that may be where Joan is. I want to say: Do not hesitate to shoot either of the bastards, but protect Sister and Mary first."

As they drew near to Mary's place they could see two sheriff's cars pulled into side driveways. Joan's car was off the road as well. They all got out and met with the Sheriff's men. Jeffery and Arthur described their plan and the reasoning behind it.

One of the men asked if they were all armed. Everyone said yes. Jeffery looked at Arthur with raised eyebrows. "I had to carry while we were in Europe. We had no idea if Diego would find us. I'm not near as good as the women or you, but I can aim and shoot." He gave a half smile.

"Okay lets go. At least the dogs are silent."

"Thank God this place is heavily treed. Okay, Arthur, I'll follow you," said Miguel.

Jeffery had Joan's phone glued to his ear as he and Romano walked between a stoop and a crawl into the yard.

Arthur and Miguel moved in the same way. "Where do you think they are?" Miguel asked.

"I'd guess in the office room over looking the waterway. That's all glass as well. Mary's room is just behind that. The next room facing us is a guest room. The living room faces east and to the north. We could be seen if anyone looked. But until Jeffery and Romano get up far enough, so they can cut over to the house, they will be the most visible."

Chapter 29

J oan hurried as fast as she could and still stay in the tree line. She kept her eyes on the windows on her side of the house. When she got opposite the carport, she quickly scooted over and under it. The dogs had stopped barking just as she got there.

She moved over by the door and put her ears up against it. She could hear Sister talking to the dogs. She scratched on the door and the dogs raced over and started barking again. Sister yelled at them to be still.

Joan tuned into her and heard her think, *"Joan is that you? If so, scratch again."*

Sister heard a faint scratch. "Good dogs. You want some water?" They gave a bark. She walked into a bathroom and turned on a faucet. *"It's that bastard Hudson, and the other one I think is Diego. They tricked their way in from the waterway. They both have guns. They are in the office room with Mary. They sent me down here to quiet the dogs. I'm the silent and dumb black help. If you understand, scratch."*

Sister walked back out to the door. She heard Joan scratch. The dogs barked and she yelled at them again. *"Joan, go back and get the car and just drive in like you were coming from the store. Don't argue. I'll tell them I heard you at the gate, and now you are coming up the drive. I know the boys are probably coming. Trust me: The more the merrier. It will keep them off guard. Yes, I have my gun. Hurry!"*

She started to talk to the dogs again. She put some food in the pans and banged about. She was going to unlock the door but was afraid that damn Hudson would find out. Finally she put her new face on again and dragged herself up the stairs, hunched over, like a tired beaten down maid would look.

Hudson was waiting at the head of the stairs and slammed the door after her. He shoved her, from behind, toward the office room. Sister stumbled and almost fell down the step into the office room, and sat in the corner chair on her right, with her head turned down away from Hudson.

"Are the dogs okay?" Mary asked.

"Yes'm." She waited a bit. "I give em some food."

"Oh, God. Whatever for? You know they only get fed at night."

"I afraid of 'em. They wouldn't hush, so I give 'em some water and food, maybe they be better. They not good dogs, at all." She was really doing everything she could to cave in on herself so Hudson wouldn't recognize her from last summer.

"Why—" Mary started to yell at her.

Diego yelled, "Shut up! Both of you!"

"I told you we just need to shoot them and get out of here," Hudson sneered.

"Shut up, Hudson. You—" He motioned at Mary, "—move over into that chair by the window. Hudson, you sit where she is."

"What the hell?" Hudson grumbled.

"Humor me. I want her turned facing me head on, not angled. I still have questions and I can tell if someone is lying if I face them head on."

"Really?" Mary said. "Then you better keep your eye on that bastard." She nodded her head at Hudson.

Sister thought, 'Oh, God, here she goes again. Going to get herself shot.'

Hudson turned in his chair and raised his gun. "Bitch, that will be your last words."

"Hudson," yelled Diego, "Put your damn gun down. Now. I told you I have more questions." He eyed him and had his gun pointed squarely at Hudson's head.

Hudson slowly lowered his gun. "Put it in your belt. Go on, put it up."

Hudson slowly put his gun in his belt. "I'm sorry Diego. I watched your brother get killed because of this bitch. I hoped someday I'd have a chance to even the score."

Mary turned her head. "What score is that, Hudson?"

Suddenly, they heard the dogs begin to bark again. "What the hell—" Diego started to say.

"That be the lady who's visiting her." She nodded at Mary. "I seen her car at the gate before I come up."

"Why the hell didn't you say something?" Hudson yelled.

Sister bowed her head, "You scared me."

"God Damn it!" Hudson yelled as he got to his feet and walked into the living room. He stared out the windows, down at the drive, as a large SUV came up the road.

"Who's that, Ms. Mary?" sneered Diego.

Mary started to stand. "No, sit. Tell me, who's that? Do you have a house guest?"

"Well, yes. She's visiting from New York."

Joan stopped the car and looked toward the carport. She could see Arthur and Miguel on the other side of the fence. She spun on her heel and walked to her right around the side yard to the front porch stairs. She didn't need Hudson coming down those inside stairs. She looked to the other fence and didn't see Jeffery.

Hudson appeared on the porch, holding the door open, as she started up the stairs. She looked up, stopped, stared and started to step back. "Hold it right there. You just come on up since you're here."

Joan held her ground, "No, I didn't know Mary had company. I'll come back." She started to turn.

"You take one step back and it'll be your last," he said as he waved the gun at her.

Joan stared up at him, gave a small nod, and started up the stairs. He backed into the dining room as she got to the porch, her arms filled with packages.

"Drop those on the floor and get in here." Joan looked at him. She thought, 'He's twitchy in his head. All over the map. Angry, frustrated, scared, nervous: damn bad mixture of emotions. I better be slow and careful not to set him off.' She carefully set the bags down and walked into the dining room. He motioned her toward the office room.

"Heres another for your collection, Diego. She looks familiar." He paused. "Yes, she was one of those at the dinner that night. If she wasn't so damn tall and with that red hair, I wouldn't have remembered."

As Joan stepped down into the office room, she looked over at Diego and stopped. He was a handsome young man. He looked more amused than angry. He was actually thinking, 'What fun this is turning out to be.'

"Good afternoon, my dear. Please join us. Sit over there on that couch in front of Mary."

Joan smiled at him, looked at Mary, who was seething with anger. No fear, just damn mad. As she stepped down into the room, right next to her, on her right sat Sister. Hunched up on a small corner chair, her face turned down and away. Trying to disappear. Joan heard, *"He hasn't recognized me yet. He still thinks I'm the dumb maid."*

Joan almost laughed out loud. *"Dumb? You're the smartest of all of us and the most dangerous."* God, she was an actress! Looking at her you would never know she was over six foot and lethal. Joan sat down and winked at Mary, who just stared.

Hudson yelled at Sister, "Go to the basement door and shut those dogs up."

Sister went to the door and quietly called the dogs, and they came up the stairs partway. She whispered to them to be still and they were. Hudson was waiting across the room as she fumbled with the lock, not turning it.

"Hurry up." He wasn't looking at her but out to the office room. He thought things were not going as he thought they should. He had to get back out there. Diego was as bad as his damn brother, who'd been a superior and arrogant ass.

Sister adjusted her gun in her pocket so she could reach it more easily, and then, bending forward, almost in a slouch, shuffled to the porch. She said in her head to Joan. *"It was damn hard not to shoot the bastard when he had his head turned, but I don't know yet what the other one is about."*

Joan couldn't help herself. She started to laugh and covered it with a cough. Mary leaned forward and said, "Do you need a glass of water, dear?" with a touch of sarcasm. She knew Sister had been talking with Joan.

"No, thank you. It's just I'm nervous around guns and he—" She nodded at Hudson, "—keeps waving one at us. I forgot his name, wasn't he in California with that man he shot?"

Hudson started to reach for his gun when Diego leaned forward yelling, "Stop, Hudson! Just sit down, damn it! Why are you letting them bait you like that?"

"Maybe he's hiding something."

"Enough," Diego said to Mary. "Before we got interrupted by this woman's—" He nodded over at Joan, "—entrance..."

Joan interrupted, "My name is Joan."

"Thank you." He nodded at Joan. "Now, Hudson, you said something about wanting to even the score. That one," he nodded at Mary, "Asked you what score it was you wanted to even. Well?"

Mary looked at Joan, said to her in her head, *"Isn't this getting interesting? I don't know if he's smarter then we think, or just a sick sociopath toying with his prey."*

"That bitch, has had it in for me for years. No matter what I tried to do here in Ponte Vedra, she always seemed to be in the way somehow. I was in London last summer, telling Santoni to let me get rid of her. He told me to leave her alone; that she was an elected official, and if anything happened to her because of me, and it led back to him, I'd be gone."

He rubbed his face and shook his head. "It was embarrassing, he told his men about it I'm sure. I was so happy when Pablo called and invited me to California with him. We looked at vineyards and land together and when he found what he wanted, it turned out this bitch owned it. No matter what he said or offered her for the land, she just laughed at him. Told him it wasn't for sale now or any time in the future."

He stopped talking for a moment, then looked at Mary. "Now you see. A lot of good that has done you. Before this afternoon is over, you won't own anything at all."

He turned to Diego, "She had horses, dressage trained. When Pablo and I visited for a private tour of the vineyard, she, her friends and two of Santoni's men were riding. Your brother was enchanted. When the tour was over, he walked over to the riding area, told her of his admiration for the vineyards and her horses.

"She barely thanked him and then turned to leave. He offered her a partnership plus a great amount of money. She stuck her nose in the air and said nothing was for sale, and rode off.

"Santoni's men just sat there, awash in arrogance, daring him to say more. Diego, Pablo was furious. It took me a long time to calm him. I wanted him to take me to the airport but he wanted dinner first. We went to a lovely place for dinner. Everything was fine. We were done and ready to leave when Santoni, his men, this bitch, and her friends came in, laughing and having a great time."

He stopped and looked out the window and shook his head. "I begged him to leave, but he said no, he wanted to just go and say a last goodbye to them." He glared at Mary.

Now, he said to himself, so far that all is accurate. Now for the fatal twist. He smiled at Mary. Now you get yours.

Chapter 30

Jeffery and Romano were still crawling toward the house when they saw Joan heading back toward the road. She had stopped by Arthur and quickly told him what Sister told her to do. She knew her phone was open to Jeffery as well. She asked if he heard her. He whispered, yes. She told him what Sister had said and what she told Joan to do. She then told all of them she was going to do what Sister told her to do.

Then, Joan ran on. The men hurried as fast as they could to get near the house. Romano, almost running in a crawl position, hissed at Jeffery as they neared the back of the house, "Duck! Here she comes."

They were in a heavily scrubbed section. Something scurried off through the grass away from them. 'God,' thought Romano, 'I pray that isn't a rattlesnake. Jeffery told me there were some on the property.'

The dogs had started to bark again as Joan drove up and stopped the car. She walked around to their side of the house. They saw her look their way as she rounded the corner of the house. As she came to the steps they saw Hudson step out on the porch landing.

They heard most of the exchange and watched Joan go up the stairs. They could see into the dining room and when Hudson turned his back and walked on to the porch, they hurried across the yard to the side of the house under the second floor walkway and porch. They heard Hudson yelling at someone to shut the dogs up. They stayed very still, backed up against the wall by the windows.

They heard Sister talk to the dogs, and then the dogs raced down the steps and she shut the door. Jeffery waited a few minutes, fearing the dogs would bark again, before turning to look into the pool and spa room, only to see Arthur smiling out at him. He waved them into the door under the porch that he had unlocked.

"How'd you get in?" He paused. "Oh; I forgot you have keys."

"Yes. Now what?"

"Sister and Joan have guns, but the first one of them who draws will get shot, and Mary too. If only one of us could get up there behind Diego. I'm sure he's sitting at Mary's desk outside her bedroom. We could shoot him from the hallway, outside her bedroom, through that room," Jeffery tentatively said.

"Then what? Hudson will shoot as many as he can before we get there. No, Jeffery, we need to wait. But if one of us could get closer without being seen, that might help later," Arthur said.

"Excuse me," Miguel said. "Let me. I'm the smallest person. I can slip around very quietly. Although I don't know Diego that well, I can assess if he is about to crack, or just playing like a cat with a mouse."

"Would he do that?" Arthur asked.

"Yes, he loves to play with people, tease, pick and annoy. He likes to see them squirm—makes him seem superior. He's not stupid. He's quick, and we still don't know if he killed that man in California. But first and foremost, he wants revenge. He will take his time and be sure he gets it."

Arthur looked at Jeffery. "Well?"

Jeffery was remembering what Sister said about trust. Didn't matter who went; shooting Diego wouldn't solve the problem of the gun in Hudson hand. "If it looks like he is going to shoot Mary, stop him."

Miguel took his shoes off. He climbed the stairs, carefully cracked the door open, and peered through the crack. He slipped in, pushing the door closed, staying low, went through the living room, and turned down the hall.

He peered through Mary's bedroom to her office. He saw Diego sitting at Mary's desk, half turned away from him. Diego leaned forward and said a loud voice, "Stop, Hudson! Just sit down, damn it..." Miguel slipped into the guest room, turned right, and opened the closet so he could duck in if he had to, then moved back to the door in time to hear Diego say "Enough!"

Miguel thought, 'Ah ha! All is not well with Hudson and Diego. Good. I'm not surprised.' He heard Diego talking with Hudson. Keeping out of sight, but still able to hear, he settled down to listen.

Hudson said, "Pablo insisted and we walked through the door of the private dining room and we found them all seated at a long table with Santoni presiding at the head, just like he owned the palace. Pablo told him he and I were leaving for the East Coast and just wanted to say goodbye. Santoni told him he was sorry he lost out on the sale of the vineyards. He said he would send him a bottle or two. Pablo got furious and turned on her." He nodded at Mary. "He asked her, 'Why did you lie to me and tell me they were not for sale?' She just stared at him and refused to answer. More angry words were exchanged that infuriated Santoni, and he reached in his belt for a gun. Pablo yelled at me to stop him. I was closer to Santoni and reached for his arm but he had already fired, shooting your brother. Someone came around the table and hit me in the head and I passed out.

"That's all I remember. When I came to I was handcuffed to a chair and having my Miranda rights read to me." He bowed his head.

Mary was avidly watching him, then she slowly began to clap her hands. "Bravo! Wonderfully performed. Did it take you long to dream up a proper script?"

"Oh, Mary, I think so," Joan said. "I was watching him. He just skimmed right along. I bet he's given this a lot of thought the past couple of days."

Hudson shifted a bit and leaned forward to his right and faced Mary. "I'm just sorry it wasn't you who got shot, but you won't have long to wait."

He turned to face Diego, "Now you can see why Santoni told you a bunch of lies. How the hell would it look if he'd just shot your brother for just insulting him? You think the authorities wouldn't have loved to get their hands on Santoni? What a huge catch he would be, the head of an international crime syndicate, and them meeting just down the road.

"I don't know how long I was out. They said I just fainted, but that's a lie. My head hurt. The back of my head ached from getting hit. They sad it was from hitting the floor. Yes, Diego, they had it all tied up by the time the authorities arrived." He bowed his head and just shook it.

"Why did they give you probation and let you go?"

"I don't know for sure. Maybe to avoid a court case. If I needed a lawyer, one who'd start asking question, that would open a can of worms. This was all decided very quickly—and don't forget Mary here—" He nodded at her. "—is very wealthy. I'm sure they don't want the landed gentry upset."

"Landed gentry, indeed. I've alway wondered who those people were. It's not an expression we use much in this country."

"What do you say, Ms. Mary?" Diego asked with a hint of sarcasm.

"Oh, for the most part, rich folks is enough. But Hudson wouldn't stoop to sounding common. He's good, I'll hand it to him. You, Diego haven't been in the country long. Your showing up must have taxed his mind. Scared him half to death, I'll bet."

Mary stopped talking and looked over at Hudson, then at Joan. "See, Joan, you're a therapist. Doesn't he look scared?"

Joan had been listening to his thoughts as he talked. He had his story straight enough, then adjusted just enough when Diego started to ask questions, to switch to arguing his case. He practiced the old 'keep it simple when you lie' routine.

But Mary was right. He was scared.

"Yes, I can see he is frightened..."

"What the hell!" yelled Hudson. "I'll show you fear, bitch," as he reached for his gun.

"No! Stop! I won't tell you one more time." Diego had rolled Mary's chair forward and was leaning forward as well, his gun aimed dead on to Hudson face.

Joan picked up on Diego's thoughts, saying to himself *'What the hell is going on with Hudson? He seems very anxious to kill them both.'*

The desk phone rang again. Diego rolled back and looked at the caller ID. "It says the Santa Rosa Police Department. Maybe you should answer this. I'd like to know what he wants." He threw the hand phone to Mary, who reached up and caught it.

"Hello."

"Mary, it's Sheriff Hall. I'm trying to reach Arthur, I have some information for you. Do you know where he is? We're sure it wasn't Diego at all."

"One minute, Sheriff." She put her hand over the mouthpiece and said, "You need to hear this. There's an extension over there in the kitchen. We both can listen. You—" She pointed at the maid. "Hand it to me."

Before Hudson could say a word, she threw the phone back to Pablo, and Sister quickly retrieved the kitchen phone and tossed it to Mary, quickly sitting down again. Hudson's head looked like it was on swivel, moving quickly between three moving parts. "Yes, I'm sorry for the interruption. Please, Sheriff Hall, go on."

Hudson, sitting forward, was staring at Diego, who never took his gun off him. Diego waved at Hudson to sit back.

"We did a time track on Ruiz; when he got to his club for lunch, who they saw him with and when he left. They said the man he had lunch with did not meet Diego's description at all. He also left the club and drove off alone. We have those times as well.

"Then the airport contacted us. They had finally found a departure time on Diego's plane. It was in the air at the same time Ruiz was having lunch at the airport. Hard to cut a man's throat from a plane.

"We finally got both his wife's permission and his Attorney's to go through his desk papers. The Attorney went over all of it with us. There were some papers about a place Ruiz was trying to sell someone. The back and forth on the correspondence demonstrated what seemed like a real gap in the offer and will-pay price. Also the man making the offer had to make a good-faith down payment that was not refundable. Apparently both parties were sure it was a done deal.

"But his attorney told us if it had been okayed, there would have been signed papers in his office. Also he noticed that each day the papers were not signed there was a penalty clause. So the buyer had to sign then and there, or he got screwed. You know Mary, Ruiz had a reputation as a sharp operator and he was not well liked by the businessmen in town.

"I'm going to call your Sheriff with this news. Will you tell Arthur? You can be somewhat relieved that it wasn't that other guy. I assume you haven't heard from him as yet."

"No, Sheriff, we haven't, and I'll have Arthur call you when he gets in. Thank you for calling." Mary disconnected the phone and laid it on the coffee table, then looked at Joan. "It seems our friend there—" She nodded at Diego. "Left Santa Rosa before Ruiz was killed."

"Well, that's a relief," Joan said. "Now we only have one mess to straighten out."

"And what would that be, Ms. Joan?" Diego asked.

"Why, the truth of this insane story he's telling." She nodded at Hudson.

"Do you really believe that makes a difference? Just because they have proven I'm not a serial killer from California?"

He shook his head, set the phone on the desk. "Nothing has changed for me. I still think his story makes some sense. It does hang together now, doesn't it?"

Chapter 31

When Sister had gone to get the kitchen phone, she noticed the door from the basement was ajar. Looking she saw some-one move. She mouthed, *Hurry!*, and waved her hand in a come-on manner.

After she left the room, Romano slipped in and ducked into the bathroom, nodding at Miguel as he entered. Mary's bathroom had a linen closet where one could stand upright. Miguel nodded at him and made a just-a-minute gesture, with one finger in the air.

With all the excitement of phones being tossed about, and the phone call, Sister had been able to get her gun out of her pocket and hidden by her thigh. Finally, she said to Joan in her thoughts, *"I have my gun in hand. One of the men may be in the hall outside Mary's bedroom door. The door to the basement was ajar. One of them probably is coming in now to hide in the bathroom."* She paused with a half-hidden smile. *"All these guns and not one safe shot to take."*

Joan started to laugh and coughed. "Need some water Ms. Joan, or was that a covered-up laugh?"

"I fear the latter, Diego. I wondered to myself what Hudson here is thinking you and Ruiz were talking about in Santa Rosa. Last year Ruiz told the police Pablo didn't much like Hudson. He told them Hudson was a gofer for Pablo just like he was for Santoni. He said Hudson tried to play the big time dealer. One night when they were at dinner together, Pablo put him in his place, since he still needed Ruiz. Your brother didn't seem to have much time for either of the men. Hired help, you know."

"You bitch!" yelled Hudson, turning toward Joan, again reaching for his gun.

"Hudson!" Diego yelled.

"No, Diego! I don't have to take any more crap off these women." He was struggling to get his gun loose when Mary tipped the lamp between them over onto Hudson's arm, knocking the gun hand down. Diego, quick as a snake, stepped forward. He glared at Mary and Joan. "Don't even think of moving a muscle. You—" He looked at Sister. "—pick up that lamp."

Sister stepped forward in front of Hudson, and picked the lamp up, setting it straight and asked Joan, 'Now?'

Joan quickly answered, "Nice move, Mary. He could have killed me, stupid bastard. If he had shot me, I do believe Diego would have killed him. He has no more tolerance for incompetent gofers than Pablo had. God knows, we don't want guns going off all over." Sister shuffled over to her chair and sat. She watched Diego step back to the desk chair. He never turned to look toward the bedroom. Diego eyed Hudson, and finally asked, "How's your current relationship with Santoni?"

"What do you mean?"

"Well it's been almost six months since my brother's death. Have you been back to London? I noticed you haven't been at any of the major meetings."

Hudson shifted in his chair, looked out the window. "Santoni is still angry that I was running around the country with Pablo. It would have been fine if it was only a vacation, but when we ran into him and his men, well, I just knew it was a bad scene. That was one of the reasons I had asked Pablo to drop me off at the airport. He insisted on dinner first."

He paused and gazed out the window. "To be honest, when Pablo insisted we go into that room, where Santoni and his men were, I was scared."

"Scared? Santoni scared you."

"Yes, he scares a lot of people. Everyone, in fact."

"Even my father?"

"No, they were like brothers. His men, we, were just hired help. 'Jump,' we jumped. If not, we would cease to exist. Santoni was rude to your brother, asking him if he was trying to steal the vineyards from him. I told you. Your brother got angry and called Santoni the thief. All hell broke loose. Pablo got shot and I got hit."

He stopped, "I know Santoni blames it all on me. So you ask, how is our relationship now? I haven't talked to the man. I sit down here doing paper work, scut work, waiting."

"You know, Diego," Mary said, "I believe he is just sitting down here in Florida waiting. Must be a tough spot to be in, Hudson. Your worst nightmare arrives, in the person of the brother of the man you shot. Now, here you are in the house of a woman who has, according to you, embarrassed you many times in the past. Truthfully, I'm surprised you are standing up as well as you are."

Joan eyed Mary. 'I wonder,' she thought, 'If Mary really knows what is going on in this man's head. Even I'm not sure. It's such a jumbled mess. I wish I could tell Sister not to shoot Diego, at least not unless she has to. She looks like she'll shoot them both in an instant. Mary is like a sister to her. She loves and admires her. I can't even reach for my gun. Mary is the only one who can bounce around. Pablo doesn't seem to mind what she does.'

Hudson groaned and started to cough as he shifted around in the chair, "I need water," he gasped. He bent over, then stood and stumbled toward the kitchen, then he turned back pulling his gun out.

Sister stood as he passed her. Seeing him turn and pull his gun, she swung at his arm and knocked it sideways as he shot. He missed Mary, the bullet going between her and Joan, cracking the window. He spun and ran for the porch door.

Diego stood and moved a step or two forward when Miguel's arm came down hard across his gun hand. The gun fell while Miguel's arm laced around Diego's's neck. "Hold it right there, Diego," he said as he pushed his gun into Diego's' head. "Step back and sit down."

Sister had started after Hudson with her gun drawn. Mary yelled, as she started into the kitchen, "Don't shoot him Sister. He's not worth the trouble it would bring you!" They both ran out on the porch watching Hudson stumbling down the stairs. He quickly looked around, saw Jeffery coming around the house, and ran for the dock.

Diego's small boat was tied, tight against the pilings, under the center walkway: hard to see if you weren't looking for it. Hudson ran out on the dock and swung down into the boat. Jeffery was running past the house, when Mary yelled, "Don't kill him, Jeffery!"

Jeffery slowed and looked back at Mary, when a shot rang out, chipping bark off a tree near him. There was a fishing boat with two men in it heading right for the dock. One of the men was yelling,

"Drop it! Drop it!" Hudson spun around, standing in the boat, raised his gun, and started to shoot at the men.

Both men unloaded their guns on him. Hudson was thrown back against the dock and then toppled into the water. Jeffery ran and grabbed a boat hook out of one of Mary's boats and caught Hudson's arm and began pulling him to the stairs leading up to the bulkhead. One of the men leaped from his boat to the dock, went down the stairs, and helped pull Hudson up the stairs to the grass.

They rolled him on to his back, and Jeffery said, "Nice shooting! He's not coming back." At least five shots had hit him, two in the head. "Call the Sheriff" he yelled up to Mary.

"He's on the way. We called him earlier," one of the officers in the boat reported. "You all are lucky he didn't hit anyone."

Jeffery walked up to the house. Mary, Sister, and Arthur were standing on the porch. "He missed you, I see," Arthur said, as Jeffery climbed the stairs. "Looked pretty close from up here."

"Yes. If Mary hadn't yelled at me, slowing me down, I may have caught one. Where is the other bastard?"

They walked through the kitchen to the office. Miguel was still standing behind Diego, who was sitting in Mary's office chair. Romano was standing nearby. Diego eyes were big and he looked shaken. He kept looking from one of the men to the other. Finally, he stared at Mary. She had returned to the chair by the window across from Joan. Sister sat on the couch by Joan, touching her hand.

Arthur sat in the chair across from him, in the one Hudson had occupied near Mary. Looking at Diego, he said, "You look like you've never seen a man killed before. That's what guns do, you know. I assume you're Diego. I've had the pleasure of speaking with your father about some business we're involved in with the Sheriff and Santoni. I surely never expected to be meeting you this way. I'm glad for your father's sake you were not killed. Losing two sons would have been terribly hard on him."

Joan had been watching Diego the whole time, and listening to his thoughts.

"I think, Arthur, he's a bit shell shocked—an old phrase, I know, but apt in this case."

Arthur turned to Mary. "Is the sheriff coming?"

"Yes, should be here soon. I was just going to suggest that Miguel and Romano take Diego to the bathroom to freshen up. Then we can all adjourn to the dining room and get this mess straightened out. I would like a glass of wine. Would that be okay, Arthur? After all, it is my home."

"Yes, dear. I'm sure we all could use one."

Joan stood. "Sister and I can do the honors. Red all around, I assume."

Mary smiled at her. "You can even use the good stuff. I'll help."

"No, you sit and talk with Arthur."

Arthur smiled at Mary. "Were you very scared?"

"Yes and no. I wasn't sure what Hudson would do. He was frantic. Joan was listening to them both. I think she thought Diego would be okay, for a while at least. He came across as just wanting to find out what was true. I think he was suspicious of Hudson.

"I must tell you Arthur: Joan and I pushed him to the brink of shooting us. I was sure if we didn't crack Hudson, then Diego could be a fatal problem for us. But Hudson was more fragile then we have ever seen him. Santoni had kept him at arm's reach for several months now—a form of torture, I'm sure.

"What was bothering me was Diego's toying with him, like a cat with a trapped mouse. I can't wait to hear what he has to say about that. He didn't like Hudson, and he treated him like he was scum. I think he was fascinated with Joan and me. He was well mannered, as were we, and Hudson hated that.

"Arthur, I'm not sad at how it ended. He really died at his own hands. I'm sure he saw no other way out than to run."

Arthur watched Mary. He was, as ever, astonished at her ability to keep it all together. When he, on one occasion, asked her how she did that, she said it stemmed from her work early in her professional life when she spent almost a year as a supervisor in a private acute psychiatric treatment center. She said it was not unusual for a patient to go off. The only safe response was to ride it out: Let them rave on and not give them an opening to physically attack you. She told him one time the verbal attack was so bad, and so scary, that after the staff got there to intervene, she went to the ladies room and found she had sweated her clothes clean through. Was she afraid?

Oh, yeah. But she knew, no matter what, don't show it.

She also told him that experience was invaluable for her. Although it wasn't repeated, there were many times when someone was angry and loudly expressing it. She wanted so badly to tell them where to go, when something clicked in, and she remembered that scene.

'Yes,' he thought, 'I'll bet, as a commissioner, this control comes in handy.'

Chapter 32

Everyone was in the dining room. The Sheriff had arrived, and his men were removing Hudson's body. He had imposed a press shutdown until they had a chance to speak with Hudson's wife. He told Arthur it was a blessing that Mary lived in Palm Valley, surrounded by trees. Also, gun shots were not unusual in the Valley.

Mary asked Sister and Joan to sit at the table with herself, Arthur, the sheriff, and Diego. The others pulled up whatever chairs they could find. Tall-stemmed glasses of wine, cheese and crackers had been set out. Diego looked less bug-eyed and more composed after he left the bathroom and sat down.

He eyed the glasses and, looking at Mary, asked, "May I?"

"Yes. You have met everyone, except Sheriff Steve Gray. Sheriff, before you start, it might be easier to bring you up to date about what happened up here before Hudson took himself off and got shot. Then I'm sure you have questions. Let's have Joan and Sister go first."

Sister introduced herself to   Diego with her full name and professional title. Diego raised his eyebrows and Sister smiled. Arthur interrupted, saying, "This is Sister's prize-winning wine you are drinking." Sister went on and described what happened before Joan's arrival.

Joan took over and described her arrival and the men sneaking up to and into the house. They all described the interplay between Mary, Joan, Hudson, and Diego. Joan did a good job of describing Hudson's growing anxiety and Mary's egging him on. She also told of Hudson wanting to kill Mary, and Diego stopping him, as well as asking him questions.

Finally, she explained it appeared that Hudson couldn't handle being questioned and challenged any more. He coughed and stumbled to the kitchen for a glass of water and reached for his gun. Sister hit his arm just as he shot at Mary and missed, hitting the window. He ran outside to the dock while shooting back at Jeffery who was chasing him. "And then your men shot him."

The Sheriff asked a few more questions, then turned to Diego. "Mr. Galeano, will you please tell me why your are here in the United States? Tell me where you went on arrival, and why. Also what were you doing here with Hudson?"

Diego looked at the wine in his glass, held it up to the light, smiled at Sister, and said, "You are indeed a Master of Wines. I salute you."

He turned to the Sheriff. "I loved and worshiped my brother Pablo. Some would say foolishly. It was hero worship. I spent all my waking hours with him. I wanted to come to the USA with him. He scoffed at me and said I was too young. Maybe some day. This time he said he would take Hudson. It was business, and I wasn't ready for serious business. It was like a slap.

"I pouted, drank and acted badly." He turned to Miguel. "Ask him. Then my father told me Pablo was dead. He told me what Santoni told him had happened. I thought I knew my brother better than they did and I didn't believe them. So I waited and finally decided that my father would not allow me to go. I went through Pablo's papers and records. I knew he would see Ruiz after picking up Hudson. So I took the plane and came by myself.

"I met with Mr. Ruiz. He showed me your vineyards, Dr. Paul, and told me what he had been told about the shooting: what Pablo had tried to do, and that Hudson had shot Pablo. He said he wasn't there but that the local Sheriff was hardnosed and wouldn't cover up for anyone." He paused and sipped more wine.

"I still didn't know what to believe, so I flew here to Florida and met with Hudson. He said Santoni shot my brother. That he was planning to steal the vineyards from Pablo, but after the shooting they must have put the sale on hold. We didn't talk much. I told him I wanted to come here to your house and confront you. Yesterday we rented a boat and scoped out the place. I saw we would need to come in by water quietly, so I got a small paddle boat, towing it, dropped Hudson, then moved off a ways anchored and paddled up under your dock. Hudson lured the dogs off toward the road. The barking got those two—" He nodded at Mary and Sister. "—to come investigate. I got behind them when they stepped out the door, and my gun persuaded them to come quietly. Sister told you the rest."

"What did you hope to accomplish?" asked the sheriff.

"I wanted the truth. I didn't like Hudson, I didn't trust him, but I couldn't believe what Santoni told my father. He was insinuating that Pablo went nuts: that he was a crazy and just went off and wanted to kill you both." He nodded at Arthur and Mary, and even Santoni. "He told my father that we were lucky to get out alive, that bastard Hudson was such a coward he shot Pablo 'cause he thought they were outnumbered. Then Hudson fainted. Hudson denied all that.

"Hudson kept getting more and more angry. Mary pushed him, and you, Joan, were watching and just talking with Mary and agreeing with everything she said or didn't say."

He stopped and looked at Joan, then Mary. No one said a thing just watched and waited him out. "It was very confusing."

"I think what bothered me the most was that none of them—" He nodded at Sister, Joan, and Mary. "—appeared at all frightened. It was strange, like they knew something I didn't know. I admit I was anxious, I didn't know who to believe and I was...scared. Maybe my fear translated itself to Hudson because he got worse and worse and wanted to kill Mary. He was very angry, and I didn't know why. I must confess, Sheriff, I don't know what I would have done if Hudson hadn't acted out and run.

"I have never shot anyone, needless to say a woman. I would like to think, I would have done all I could to stop Hudson from shooting any of the women. But I cannot say I would have shot him first. I don't think I was capable of that level of thinking." He stopped and looked at Joan. "You knew that, didn't you?"

Joan quietly nodded at him, then smiled. "But you see, Diego, both Sister and I were armed. Our first priority was always Mary. I'm sure Sister would have taken Hudson out, and while you were making up your mind I'd have shot you. Hudson just surprised us all when he cut and ran. Then turned in his hatred to take out Mary, who he thought was an old enemy of his."

"Yes," Sister said in agreement. "I did what I could to deflect his aim. I saw Miguel grab Diego from behind. He was behind him in Mary's bedroom. He had to stay hidden for the same reasons. No one wanted to set you or Hudson off, and get Mary or any of us shot."

Diego sat there looking at his glass and moving the wine around in the bowl. Finally he asked Miguel, "Was Pablo different then the man I thought he was?" He waited and watched Miguel. "You don't need to be afraid to tell me."

"Diego," Romano interrupted, "Miguel did not know your brother well at all. I was told he did not work with him or around him. He is here because he was the only senior man available to come with us who knew you at all. There are others in Spain who can better answer that question, but from what I saw of him at the vineyards, when we were riding the horses, I would say he was a man who was used to getting whatever he wanted. He did not take kindly to being told no. Mary tried to tell him as nicely as possible that the vineyards were not for sale, as did Arthur.

"He refused to accept that, and Mary was left with no alternative but to turn and ride away. Pablo, was I think, insulted that she had turned her back on him, but he left her no choice. There were several of us standing around, which I'm sure made it worse for him. He turned and walked away to his car. Had he just left the area, all would have been over, and he could have continued his search for a new vineyard."

Diego listened. "You and these other men—" He waved at them all. "—were there as well?"

"Yes."

"I see." He looked around the room."He could never have scared Mary into selling with all of you standing with her."

"No, Diego. I do not, and did not, need them standing with me. Your brother didn't bother me at all. I am my own woman. Do not ever think otherwise."

"We sure know that!" said the Sheriff, laughing. "I have known this woman for many years. She is a ardent fisherwoman. She has a gun on the boat when she fishes alone. The one time I know of, when she was out in her boat and was approached by two men who meant her harm, she told me she reached for her gun and it wasn't there, so she loaded her flare gun and waved it at them and they left in a hurry.

"We captured them some time later and they told me that was *one crazy lady*. They knew she would not have hesitated to pull the trigger on that flare gun. When she was elected Commissioner, I insisted she take a gun course and get a permit to carry. She grumbled, but knew it was the smart thing to do.

"Now, Mary, I have a few more questions to ask Diego, so I will walk him outside with me. I want your people to suggest, considering what he has done, what I should do with him."

He and Diego walked out the door.

Chapter 33

"What a clever man, your sheriff," Sister said, and smiled at Mary.

"Is that what you would call it? Seems to me to be classical political buck passing."

Arthur cleared his throat, trying not to laugh. "What is that old saying? It takes one..."

"Very funny. Well, since he said he wants my people to decide—" She looked around. "—I guess he means you are my people, so let's get started. Jeffery, you were not in the house and had not seen or heard Diego until now. Based on what everyone said so far, and what he said, give me an opinion."

"You mean other than he should burn in hell for holding you, Sister, and Joan at gun point and terrorizing you?"

"Yes, please. Other than that." There were a few smiles and nods at that remark.

"He is a victim of his upbringing: a father who seemed too busy to pay attention to what was happening to his sons. The only role model Diego had was a arrogant, self-indulgent, borderline psychopath, who luckily didn't seem to give him much time either. A pretty thin straw to hang on to. I can see where he felt he needed to find out what happened to Pablo, since he didn't believe his father.

"Too bad he ran into that damn Hudson. He had no way of knowing how close Hudson was to cracking up himself. Santoni shouldn't have left him to sit down here, brooding. I'm sure that did more to make him crazier than he already was. I will tell Santoni that when I next see him. Should have just put him away like you do a sick dog. As for Diego's future I will leave that in the hands of the more learned and understanding souls sitting around this table."

"Romano?"

"I didn't know Diego. I only met his brother once in Spain, and at the Vineyard. From that exposure, I agree with Jeffery, however, let me add: Hudson will not be missed." He nodded at Miguel.

Miguel nodded his head, "I did not know Diego well at all. I did not socialize with him in Spain: different class. I have no more to add. I will do whatever you all tell me to do. Romano and Jeffery, I want to thank you for trusting me to help you. I would not have liked to be the one to shoot Diego, but I would not have allowed him to harm any of you." He bowed his head and Jeffery and Romano patted his back.

Mary nodded at Mac. He smiled at her. "Mary, I agree with Jeffery. I treasure you three women. I'd have killed him myself if he had harmed any of you."

"Sister, again, thank you for saving my life." Sister nodded and smiled at Mary.

"It was my pleasure. I wanted to shoot that man Hudson from the start. He was a very nasty piece of work. Joan is right: I would have shot Hudson in a second if he had moved to kill you, and Diego as well.

"However, I must say Diego acted as a gentleman as best the conditions allowed. He was polite, never profane, never threatening, and did control Hudson as best he could. I think he was surprised at Hudson's behavior. He seemed to be doubting Hudson's story about what happen when his brother got shot. He did not want to believe that his brother was at fault, but Hudson had him confused. This may sound strange but I did feel that Diego was confused, and felt he had been dropped into a nightmare of his own making.

"He did not know how to get out of it. You and Joan kept the pressure on. He was not a trusting man, this Hudson. In retrospect, we should not be surprised that he wanted to kill Mary and run. Mary told me her history with him over the years. Altogether, it was too much for him. Actually too much for Diego as well. He is a very young man who was in way over his head."

Mary turned to Joan. "Mixed bag, isn't it?"

"Everything has been laid out clearly, as each person sees it—not too many with reservations, but no suggestions offered."

"Would you send him home?"

"Not without some psych help. I don't know what is available in Spain. But I would not advise that he go back there. The situation with the father will be too tough. No, Mary, he should not go home. He needs to have some support, control, and structure."

"Is he as confused as he presents?"

"Oh, yes! Without question. He is very vulnerable now. I think he will do what we recommend. But to repeat myself he will need support. A structure he can function in while he finds who he is."

"If he doesn't agree?"

"Then toss his ass in jail," Jeffery said.

"Arthur?"

"I agree with Joan and Jeffery. Further, I suggest he go to England and be but under the supervision of Santoni. I don't mean close personal contact, but like a paroled sponsorship. I don't mean to put you in the hot seat, Romano, but you might act as a go-between. Can we get him into a school or an academy of some sort?"

"I don't know what his educational background is. We will have to ask him. I, too, agree with both Arthur and Joan, but you will have to talk with Santoni, and get Diego's complete consent. Since Santoni is so close to the father he may be agreeable, if Diego will cooperate."

"Okay, we can investigate that. How about we have him up here with the sheriff, Arthur, Joan, and I. Romano, go and get him and bring him in. Arthur, will you explain to the Sheriff, before he comes in, what our thinking is? The boys and Mac can sit in the office with Sister. Sister, if you will, sit near the door where you can hear but not be seen." Sister nodded.

After the men left Mary turned to the women. "I know this seems a bit convoluted, but I don't know how else to do this."

Sister patted her arm, "Let it play out, Mary. You're being more than fair. Like Jeffery said: 'be easier to toss his ass in jail.'"

When everyone was seated, the sheriff turned to Mary. "Do you have a suggestion about what we should do with this young man?" He nodded at Diego. "As you must know, we have grounds to lock him up: holding you at gunpoint and terrorizing you and your friends. He would be put away for a while. Even his father couldn't help him."

"Yes. Thank you, Sheriff. We have all discussed this and the consensus is for Joan to explain what she has observed, and what she thinks would help Diego in this mess he has created."

Joan sat very still and just looked at Mary. Mary said to her in her mind, *"Well, my dear, when an expert is needed one would be a fool not to get their help."*

Joan made a tiny nod, adding a smirk, then looked at Diego. "Well, young man, you have made a bonkers of this, haven't you?"

Diego looked at her, bowed his head and nodded. "We have all talked about what can be done with you, beside the obvious option of jail. You haven't a clue how you got into this mess. In fact, if I'm not mistaken, you never intended this to have gone so far."

"No ma'am. I... I'm so sorry. I didn't know Hudson. I, I didn't much like him when I met him, but I didn't know what to do to find out the truth. My brother was killed. I didn't understand how that could have happened. Hudson told me a story, but it seemed strange, so I thought I just go find out for myself." He stopped and just looked at her.

"You have been told by us what happened. What reason would we have to lie? Your brother came damn close to shooting a number of us and killing Dr. Paul. We did not know your brother, or your father for that matter." He started to speak, but Joan held her hand up. "No Diego. I know you are very confused and deeply disturbed. We do not think it would be in your best interest, or anyone else's, for you to be sent home to your father.

"Nor do we think it would help you at this time to sit in jail. However we cannot just let you go off in the world in the mental condition you are in. We are prescribing for you a series of therapy sessions, combined with residence at a good school in England, all under the supervision of Santoni. You need not spend time with him, but he will be your probation person. Do you understand me?"

Diego looked both relieved and befuddled. "You think I am in need of psychiatric help? As well as an education?"

"Yes. We don't know how much schooling you've had, but you need to be prepared to go on in this world without your father's help. After your therapist has released you, and you have developed the necessary skill set to operate in this world, then you can decide what the future may hold for you.

"Your father, I understand is involved in the wine business: the growing, making and distribution. He is also involved in other businesses. Whichever of these interests you care about will be waiting for you, or you may discover you have developed other interests entirely.

"You may not return to Spain until your therapist releases you from both the need for treatment and education. I will remain in contact with your therapist, Santoni, and Sheriff Gray. If at any time you wish a conference with the three of us you may ask. Your father will be held accountable for the expenses of the therapist, the school, your living expenses, and my expenses as a consultant.

"These are the conditions of your parole, should Sheriff Gray agree. How long they last is dependent on your progress. Do you and any of the rest of you have any questions at this time?"

Gray smiled at Joan and then asked Mary if there was any of that wonderful wine left.

Chapter 34

Everyone had left. Despite all that had happened, it was still mid-afternoon. Jeffery and Miguel took Diego to the Casa Monica hotel in St. Augustine to settle his bill and check him out. They then took him to the Sheriff's office to be fingerprinted and have his statistics noted for the record.

The Sheriff's top man in the Ponte Vedra area, a Lieutenant, took over the chore of notifying Hudson's wife of his death. He was told to play down the people who were there: Call it case of mistaken identity, mistaken location. He was to tell her when the home owner yelled at Hudson, who was trying to break in, he started to run. The homeowner had called the police. When Hudson saw the police, he shot at them, and they shot back and killed him. He suggested the wife call Hudson's boss.

Mac, Arthur, and Romano left for the Sheriff's office to call and talk with Santoni. Sister went to the hotel to make room arrangements for Diego to join the men there. She arranged for a suite for the three: Diego, Miguel, and Romano. Then she asked the hotel if they could suggest and arrange for a caterer for nine at Mary's. They had all agreed they did not want to eat out. The hotel knew just who to ask, and put her together with them via phone and she made arrangements for dinner to be sent to Mary's, and ready by eight that evening.

Joan sat with Mary after everyone left. Mary fixed them a snack and settled in the office. She smiled at Joan. "Let's agree you will put your screens up while we talk. I don't want to sit here and have to think and rethink everything I say."

Joan threw her head back and laughed. "Sister is right. You are a jewel! You don't pull punches and sneak around at all, do you?"

"Oh, I can if I have to, but not with friends. If I did, they wouldn't be worth much as friends, now, would they? Anyhow, it has been a tiring and even stressful afternoon. Be nice to just sit here and talk with you without walls up all over."

"I agree. It won't be hard—I don't just hear the whole world, you know. I have to tune in, I guess you could call it. And yes, I'm a bit tired mentally as well. I must tell you we worked very well together. If I didn't know better I would have thought you were in my head like Sue."

"Well it wasn't hard. We were actually talking to each other on the pretense of talking to everyone. Even Sister kept up. Good friends who like each other can do that. Also, it was easy. I was really interested in what we all were saying and what the hell was going on with Diego. I didn't sense any evil in him. Like you suggested, he just seemed very confused."

"Hum." Joan nodded. "I must say, though, I was concerned about Hudson. He was mean. He wanted to hurt us—especially you, but actually any and all of us. I don't think he liked women, or shall I say, respected them, at all. He saw Sister as dirt. If she hadn't acted so subservient he would have hit out at her just for the hell of it. As it was she didn't exist for him. A very nasty piece of work, he was."

"I want to thank you for being so gracious and quick on your feet when I dumped Diego in your lap."

"Oh, yeah, then tried to smooth it over with that expert remark."

She smiled. "But, Mary, it wasn't that difficult. Arthur had already worked it out. I had only to tell it to Diego. Also, while I was talking, it all came together. I was the logical person to be the consultant. Anyone else, we would have had to explain, say, to a therapist, who these people were. Plus, I have the added advantage of being able to tell if Diego is about to jump ship. I will also help pick out the therapist, and make it clear they are to report to me directly."

"I think it will work out very well. I'm so glad you went to Europe with Arthur, Mac, and Sister. When did you decide to go?"

"At Christmas." Joan looked out the window for the longest time. She half smiled. "You remember, I went to California to finish the editorial work on the book. Sister joined me in San Francisco. We shopped, dined, and talked." She again looked out the window for a bit. "We told each other our stories. It was like finding a long-lost sister: a missing part that just slipped into place"

Mary sat quietly as Joan told her. "Those parts meshed over the rest of the holiday. Going to Europe with her was just logical, again like we had always been together. We worked very well together.

"I knew nothing about what we were doing concerning wine, but I'm not stupid. When all the puzzle pieces of creating the wines were revealed, Sister just slipped them together. The champagne part was difficult, and I sensed how frustrated Sister was getting. Can you imagine finding three different grapes and mixing them to perfection? Then he mentioned he made a had a blanc de blanc, using it as the main base. From then on it was easy! Lucky, too..." She went on then told the rest of the story. She quickly finished with the port.

"Will they all turn out like you want?"

"Oh yes. Sister is a master, never fear. Mac will make the ports, now that he knows which of his grapes will work. You know, Mary, it will be the crown of his career, and the champagnes the finished product of Sister's. A very successful trip and adventure, really."

"Now what?"

Joan looked out the window, smiling. "I think Mary, my friend, the continuing of a lovely and loving relationship."

CPSIA information can be obtained
at www.ICGtesting.com
Printed in the USA
FSOW02n0130171016
26185FS